SCHOLASTIC

2022

BOOK OF WORLD RECORDS

BY
CYNTHIA O'BRIEN
ABIGAIL MITCHELL
MICHAEL BRIGHT
DONALD SOMMERVILLE
ANTONIA VAN DER MEER

If you purchased this book without a cover, you should be aware that this book is stolen property. It was reported as "unsold and destroyed" to the publisher, and neither the author nor the publisher has received any payment for this "stripped book."

Copyright © 2021 by Scholastic Inc.

All rights reserved. Published by Scholastic Inc., *Publishers since 1920.* SCHOLASTIC and associated logos are trademarks and/or registered trademarks of Scholastic Inc.

Due to this book's publication date, the majority of statistics are current as of May 2021. The publisher does not have any control over and does not assume any responsibility for author or third-party websites or their content.

No part of this publication may be reproduced, stored in a retrieval system, or transmitted in any form or by any means, electronic, mechanical, photocopying, recording, or otherwise, without written permission of the publisher. For information regarding permission, write to Scholastic Inc., Attention: Permissions Department, 557 Broadway, New York, NY 10012.

This book was created and produced by Toucan Books Limited.
Text: Cynthia O'Brien, Abigail Mitchell, Michael Bright, Donald Sommerville, Antonia van der Meer
Designer: Lee Riches
Editor: Anna Southgate
Proofreader: Richard Beatty
Index: Marie Lorimer
Toucan would like to thank Clan O'Day for picture research

ISBN 978-1-338-76804-6

10 9 8 7 6 5 4 3 2 1   21 22 23 24 25

Printed in the U.S.A. 40

First printing, 2021

CONTENTS

- 1 — 4
- 2 — 22
- 3 — 46
- 4 — 62
- 5 — 84
- 6 — 110
- 7 — 154
- 8 — 182
- 9 — 236

276 Index
283 Photo Credits
285 Scholastic Summer Reading Challenge

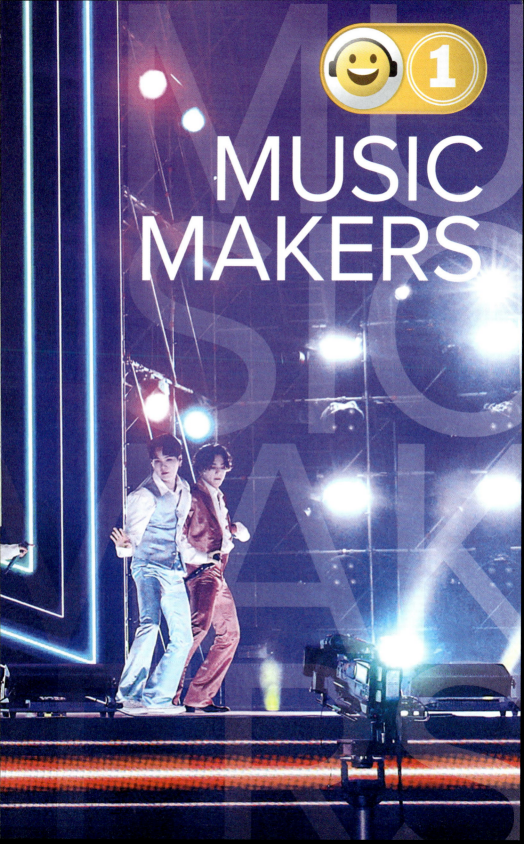

STRIKE A POSE
Harry Styles embraces the lace

In November 2020, singer, actor, and former One Direction member Harry Styles made waves as *Vogue* magazine's first-ever solo male cover star. Known for his love of flamboyant silk suits, he posed in various androgynous looks for the magazine, drawing outrage from some quarters for breaking with traditional gender roles. Styles replied to his critics by posting a snap of himself in a pastel blue ruffled suit, and the tongue-in-cheek caption "Bring back manly men."

 Music Makers

trending

#SHANTYTOK
Sailor song revival

An unexpected music style made a comeback during lockdown when Scottish postal worker Nathan Evans posted a TikTok of himself singing a centuries-old sea shanty—a rhythmic song sung by sailors. "Soon May the Wellerman Come" sparked an international singalong, spawned countless duets, and revived a traditional genre. Not only did Evans ignite a popular TikTok trend, but his full version of "Wellerman" climbed to no. 1 in the UK Top 40 charts in January 2021.

STILL ICONIC
The new queen of Twitter

Soul singer Dionne Warwick, who turned eighty in December 2020, went viral on Twitter last year with some hilarious roasts of some of our favorite stars—from asking the Weeknd where the missing "e" is to calling herself "Dionne the Singer" in the style of Chance the Rapper.

BREAKUP ANTHEM
"Drivers License" goes viral

Seventeen-year-old singer-songwriter and Disney actress Olivia Rodrigo made headlines in January 2021 with the release of her breakup ballad "Drivers License." Skyrocketing to no. 1 in the UK and US, it broke the Spotify record for most streams of a song in a week—with 76.1 million in the US alone.

"DYNAMITE" COMES OUT WITH A BANG
New BTS single breaks records

"Dynamite," a single by K-pop septet BTS, exploded onto the music scene in August, setting multiple records. The music video, which shows the group dancing in various retro American sets—a donut shop, an ice cream van, a basketball court, a disco—was the most viewed music video in twenty-four hours on YouTube and had the "most simultaneous viewers for a music video on YouTube Premieres."

Music Makers

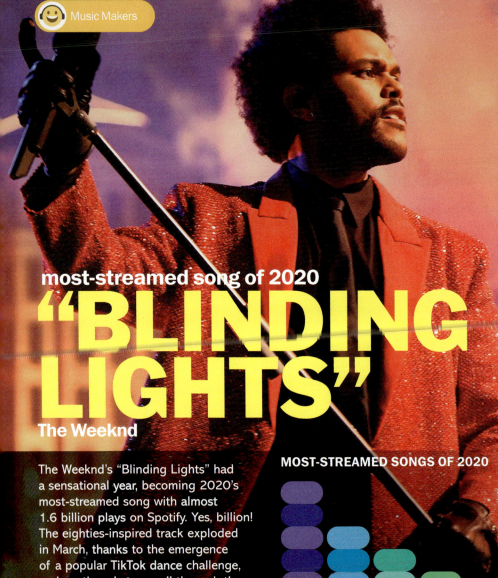

most-streamed song of 2020

"BLINDING LIGHTS"

The Weeknd

The Weeknd's "Blinding Lights" had a sensational year, becoming 2020's most-streamed song with almost 1.6 billion plays on Spotify. Yes, billion! The eighties-inspired track exploded in March, thanks to the emergence of a popular TikTok dance challenge, and continued strong all through the summer. After the Weeknd lit up the halftime show at the 2021 Super Bowl, his chaotically energetic performance of the song was turned into a popular reaction GIF showcasing the best close-ups of the Canadian singer stumbling around in a maze of lights.

MOST-STREAMED SONGS OF 2020

The Weeknd, "Blinding Lights"
Tones and I, "Dance Monkey"
Roddy Ricch, "The Box"
Imanbek and SAINt JHN, "Roses (Imanbek Remix)"
Dua Lipa, "Don't Start Now"

top-selling album
FOLKLORE
Taylor Swift

Taylor Swift shocked fans in 2020 with not one, but two surprise album drops: *folklore*, which was released in July, and its sister album *evermore* (released in December). Both captivated the hearts and ears of fans around the world with a more pared down, folksy sound from the country star turned pop princess.

It's no surprise that *folklore* was the top-selling album of the year, with Swift's eighth studio album selling 1.2 million copies. *Evermore* also made the top ten, with 270,000 copies sold. The year 2020 marks Taylor's fifth top seller, after *Fearless* (2009), *1989* (2014), *Reputation* (2017), and *Lover* (2019).

 Music Makers

most-liked video on YouTube
DESPACITO

With more than forty-three million likes, "Despacito" is the most-liked video on YouTube. The Puerto Rican dance track by Luis Fonsi feat. Daddy Yankee proved a hot favorite in 2017 and was the first music video to notch up four, five, and then six billion views on YouTube, before hitting an amazing seven billion in October 2020. Even now, the video is played an average of 1.4 million times a day! That's not to say it's everybody's favorite. According to YouTube's stats, the video also ranks as no. 15 in the most-disliked videos on the channel with an impressive five million dislikes!

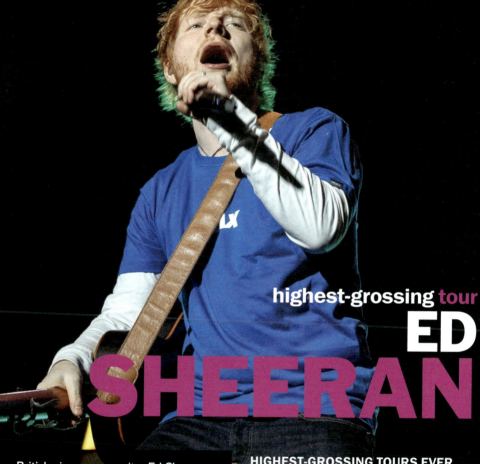

highest-grossing tour
ED SHEERAN

British singer-songwriter Ed Sheeran has the highest-grossing tour of all time, surpassing those of U2, the Rolling Stones, Guns N' Roses, and Coldplay. Sheeran's tour for his album ÷ (*Divide*) grossed $775.6 million, making it the biggest moneymaker ever for a musical tour. Sheeran's impressive title is no doubt helped by the fact that the tour stretched for longer than two years, beginning in Turin, Italy, in March 2017 and ending in Ipswich, England, in August 2019. By the time it was over, Sheeran had visited forty-three countries and had performed before 8.5 million people.

HIGHEST-GROSSING TOURS EVER
Revenue in millions of US dollars

Ed Sheeran, Divide: **775.6**

U2, 360°: **736**

Guns N' Roses, Not in This Lifetime . . . : **584**

The Rolling Stones, A Bigger Bang: **558**

Coldplay, A Head Full of Dreams: **523**

11

Music Makers

DRAKE
first rapper to top Billboard 100 chart

Drake released his album *If You're Reading This It's Too Late* through iTunes on February 12, 2015. The digital album sold 495,000 units in its first week and entered the *Billboard* 100 at no. 1, making Drake the first rap artist ever to top the chart. The album also helped Drake secure another record: the most hits on the *Billboard* 100 at one time. On March 7, 2015, Drake had fourteen hit songs on the chart, matching the record the Beatles have held since 1964. Since releasing his first hit single, "Best I Ever Had," in 2009, Drake has seen many of his singles go multiplatinum, including "Hotline Bling," which sold 41,000 copies in its first week and had eighteen weeks at no. 1 on the *Billboard* 100.

top group/duo
BTS

Billboard officially named K-pop megastar band BTS the top group of 2020 following another year of global domination. At the *Billboard Music Awards*, the septet took home the "top social" award for the fourth year in a row, thanks in part to their infamous "ARMY" of dedicated fans around the world. According to Forbes, the seven-member boy band also claimed five out of ten of the spots in 2020's top World Songs chart, with "Stay" from *BE* at no. 1, followed by "Life Goes On" (no. 2), "Filter" (no. 3), "My Time" (no. 9), and "Euphoria" (no. 10).

Music Makers

top-selling recording group
THE BEATLES

TOP-SELLING RECORDING GROUPS IN THE UNITED STATES
Albums sold in millions

- 183 — The Beatles
- 156 — Garth Brooks
- 146.5 — Elvis Presley
- 120 — Eagles
- 111.5 — Led Zeppelin

The Beatles continue to hold the record for the best-selling recording group in the United States with 183 million albums sold. The British band recorded their first album in September 1962 and made their Billboard debut with "I Want to Hold Your Hand." Before breaking up in 1969, the group had twenty number-one songs and recorded some of the world's most famous albums, including *Sgt. Pepper's Lonely Hearts Club Band*.

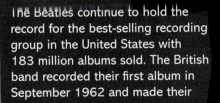

14

longest-ever music video
"LEVEL OF CONCERN"
Twenty One Pilots

Twenty One Pilots collaborated with their fans in 2020 to create the longest music video ever! The official video for their hit "Level of Concern" lasted for 177 days, 16 hours, 10 minutes, and 25 seconds, with the song constantly looping as fan-made video submissions were played on the live stream. The band announced the end of its "never-ending" stream by joking that the only way it would stop was for the power to go out . . . followed by a video of band member Joshua Dun overloading his Christmas tree with lights!

top-earning female singer
ARIANA
GRANDE

TOP-EARNING FEMALE SINGERS
In millions of US dollars

72 — Ariana Grande
63.5 — Taylor Swift
53 — Billie Eilish
47.5 — Jennifer Lopez
47 — P!nk

Legend:
- Ariana Grande
- Taylor Swift
- Billie Eilish
- Jennifer Lopez
- P!nk

Music Makers

Ariana Grande had a super-successful 2020, which included the release of her live tour documentary *Excuse Me, I Love You*, meeting and getting engaged to partner Dalton Gomez, and breaking the record for most songs to debut at no. 1 on the *Billboard* Hot 100. It's no wonder that Ariana topped off the year as the world's top-earning female singer, raking in $72 million. A huge portion of those earnings came from the Sweetener world tour, chronicled in *Excuse Me, I Love You*.

From March through July 2019, rapper Lil Nas X's "Old Town Road" spent seventeen weeks in the no. 1 spot, pushing past "Despacito" from Luis Fonsi and Mariah Carey's "One Sweet Day," each of which spent sixteen weeks at the top of the charts. Lil Nas X's real name is Montero Hill, and he is from Atlanta, Georgia. He recorded the song himself, and people first fell in love with the catchy tune on the app TikTok. "Old Town Road" made it to the country charts, but it was later dropped for not being considered a country song. Disagreements about its genre only fueled interest in the song, however, and it subsequently hit no. 1. The song was then remixed and rerecorded with country music star Billy Ray Cyrus, whose wife, Tish, encouraged him to become involved.

longest-running no. 1 single
"OLD TOWN ROAD"

Music Makers

act with the most Country Music Awards

GEORGE STRAIT

"King of Country" George Strait won his first Country Music Awards (CMAs) in 1985 for Male Vocalist of the Year and Album of the Year. Since then, Strait has won an amazing twenty-three CMAs, including Entertainer of the Year in 2013. The country music superstar has thirty-three platinum or multiplatinum albums, and he holds the record for the most platinum certifications in country music. George Strait was inducted into the Country Music Hall of Fame in Nashville, Tennessee, in 2006.

musician with the most MTV Video Music Awards
BEYONCÉ

The queen of pop, Beyoncé, is the winningest VMA artist ever. She won eight MTV Video Music Awards in 2016 alone, pushing her ahead of Madonna's twenty VMA trophies and setting a new record of twenty-five VMA wins. The music video for "Formation," from Beyoncé's visual album *Lemonade*, won five awards, including the coveted prize for Video of the Year. With eight Moon Person trophies from eleven nominations, Beyoncé tied the record for the most VMA wins in one year by a female solo artist, also held by Lady Gaga.

MUSICIANS WITH THE MOST MTV VIDEO MUSIC AWARDS

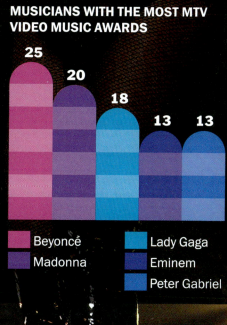

- Beyoncé — 25
- Madonna — 20
- Lady Gaga — 18
- Eminem — 13
- Peter Gabriel — 13

Music Makers

first all-Spanish album to top the *Billboard* 200 chart

EL ÚLTIMO TOUR DEL MUNDO
Bad Bunny

Bad Bunny's debut album *El Último Tour del Mundo* (*The Last Tour in the World*) made music history in 2020, landing the top spot on *Billboard*'s 200 album chart. It's the first time in *Billboard*'s sixty-four-year history that an album performed entirely in Spanish has reached no. 1. The album, featuring a mix of Latin trap, reggaeton, and ska-punk was one of three albums released by the Puerto Rican rapper, singer, and songwriter in 2020. His second album, *YHLQMDLG*, had reached no. 2 in the chart in February. And that's not all! Bad Bunny, whose birth name is Benito Martínez Ocasio, ended 2020 as Spotify's most-streamed artist of the year, amassing a staggering 8.3 billion streams.

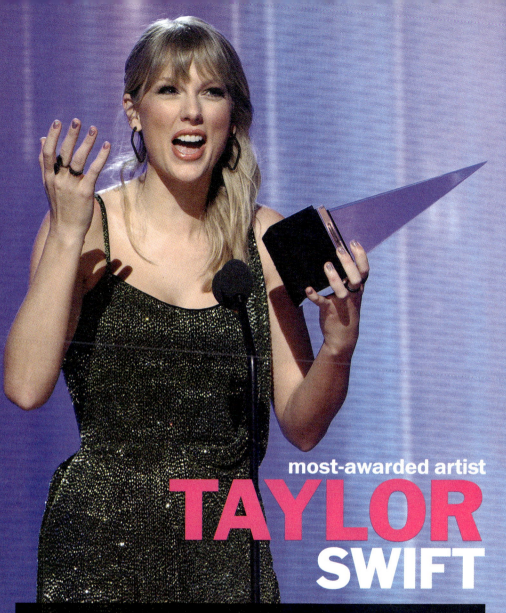

most-awarded artist
TAYLOR SWIFT

In 2020, Taylor Swift maintained her title as the most-awarded artist ever at the prestigious American Music Awards. Three wins—for Artist of the Year, Favorite Music Video, and Favorite Female Artist—bring Swift's AMA total to thirty-two. This breaks her own record of twenty-nine AMAs, set when she won six honors and the 2019 awards, including Artist of the Decade. With the next most-awarded artist being Michael Jackson, with twenty-four awards, it looks as if it could be some time before Swift's record is beaten . . . by anyone, but her, that is! Among other awards, Swift's *folklore* won a Grammy for Album of the Year, making her the first female artist to win the best album award three times.

STAGE & SCREEN

2

History was made at the Oscars in 2020 when the South Korean film *Parasite* became the first-ever Best Picture winner in a language other than English. *Parasite*'s Bong Joon Ho also took home the awards for Best Original Screenplay and Best Director. Although *Parasite* won big, the director pointed out after the ceremony that there are many other spectacular non-English films out there—for people who can get over the "one-inch-tall barrier of subtitles."

OSCARS GO GLOBAL
Parasite wins Best Picture

Stage & Screen

trending

REST IN POWER
Most-liked tweet ever

Black Panther star Chadwick Boseman passed away in August 2020 from colon cancer. His passing was announced on Twitter by his team in an emotional message that broke records for the outpouring of grief that followed: 2.1 million retweets; 924,500 quote tweets; 165,600 comments; and 7.5 million likes. In under twenty-four hours it became the most-liked tweet ever, with Twitter calling it "a tribute fit for a king."

ACE PRIDE
SpongeBob flies the flag

Nickelodeon celebrated Pride in 2020 by posting pictures of characters from the LGBTQIA+ community, including Korra from *The Legend of Korra* and, surprising many, SpongeBob SquarePants! In articles dating back to 2005, creator Stephen Hillenburg has said that, like real sea sponges, SpongeBob is asexual! Members of the community were over the moon to see asexuality recognized on the LGBTQIA+ spectrum by a major children's programming network.

GRINT ON THE GRAM
Fastest to 1M Instagram followers

It took Rupert Grint only four hours and one minute to reach one million followers on Instagram. The *Harry Potter* star delighted fans when he joined the platform in November 2020 with an adorable picture of his baby daughter, Wednesday G. Grint, and a throwback profile pic of himself with costar Dame Maggie Smith (Minerva McGonagall).

EXPANDING UNIVERSE
MCU takes to the small screen

With the launch of *WandaVision* on Disney+, the Marvel Cinematic Universe kicked off its Phase Four in spectacular style. The franchise looked set to dominate 2021 with a slew of films and TV shows brimming with characters old and new. *The Falcon and the Winter Soldier* followed *WandaVision* on Disney+, while *Black Widow*—the first of several movies—saw the Avengers' heroine confront her past. It was an impressive comeback after more than a year without releases following the end of Phase Three.

Stage & Screen

THE SIMPSONS

longest-running scripted TV show in the United States

In 2020, The Simpsons entered a record thirty-second season, continuing to hold the title of longest-running American sitcom, cartoon, and scripted prime-time television show in history. The animated comedy, which first aired in December 1989, centers on the antics and everyday lives of the Simpson family. Famous guest stars who have made appearances over the years range from Stephen Hawking to Kelsey Grammer and Ed Sheeran (as Lisa's new crush). Fox has renewed the show for the upcoming thirty-third season, too.

26

SCHITT'S CREEK

TV show with the most Emmy Awards for a comedy in a single year

Dan and Eugene Levy's hit comedy finished its sixth and final season in 2020, much to the dismay of its fans. However, the Canadian show's successful run was honored on the awards circuit, breaking records by taking home nine Emmys—a new Emmy record for a comedy in a single year! Main cast members Eugene Levy, Catherine O'Hara, Dan Levy, and Annie Murphy won Emmys for Outstanding Lead Actor, Lead Actress, Supporting Actor, and Supporting Actress in a comedy series, respectively, and the show also picked up wins for outstanding writing, casting, costumes, and directing.

27

Stage & Screen

most popular game show
JEOPARDY!

All four episodes of *Jeopardy! The Greatest of All Time* made it onto Nielsen's list of 100 Most-Watched Prime Time Telecasts of 2020, making it the year's most popular game show. The tournament featured former champions competing against each other for a million-dollar grand prize. The year 2020 also brought the end of Alex Trebek's decades-long hosting gig, which included 8,000 episodes across thirty-seven seasons. Trebek, who announced a cancer diagnosis in 2019, passed away on November 8, 2020, a week after he filmed his last episode for the show.

28

most-popular original Netflix show of 2020

THE QUEEN'S GAMBIT

Checkmate! Anya Taylor-Joy's Beth Harmon captured the hearts of viewers worldwide as *The Queen's Gambit* became Netflix's most binge-watched original show in 2020. Taylor-Joy also enjoyed some personal success, winning a Golden Globe in 2021 for her role. Based on the 1983 book by Walter Tevis, the show details a young orphan's journey to becoming a chess prodigy as she faces her troubled past and pushes back against 1960s-typical sexism. According to figures released by Netflix, *The Queen's Gambit* was Netflix's no. 1 original series in sixty-three countries and was apparently watched by 63 million accounts.

Stage & Screen

most-watched television broadcast of 2020
SUPER BOWL LIV

The most-watched television broadcast of 2020 was *Super Bowl LIV*. A whopping 102 million viewers tuned in on February 2, to watch the Kansas City Chiefs beat the San Francisco 49ers 31–20. That's four million more than the TV audience for the 2019 Super Bowl. In a year when many sports events were delayed or canceled owing to the COVID-19 pandemic, football appears to have fared pretty well. According to *Variety*, eight of the ten most-viewed TV shows of 2020 were football-related. The Oscars and a post–football season episode of *The Masked Singer* were the only other programs to claim a top 10 spot.

highest-paid child actor
MILLIE BOBBY BROWN

In 2020, British actress Millie Bobby Brown reportedly earned $350,000 per episode for *Stranger Things* Season 3, making her the highest-paid actor under age eighteen. Her net worth is now reported at around $10 million, thanks to her role in 2020's *Enola Holmes*, modeling work, and various brand endorsements. Brown, a UNICEF Goodwill Ambassador, has donated some of her earnings to help frontline workers during the COVID-19 crisis, and she has raised money for the Olivia Hope Foundation with her makeup line for teens, Florence by Mills. Is there anything this girl can't do?

Stage & Screen

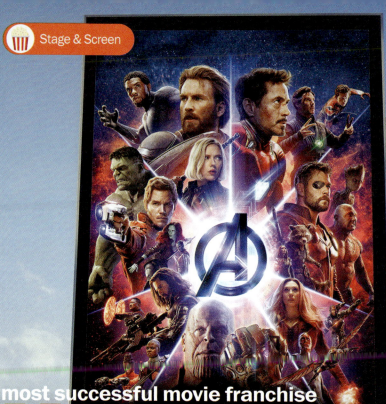

most successful movie franchise
MARVEL CINEMATIC UNIVERSE

MOST SUCCESSFUL MOVIE FRANCHISES
Total worldwide gross, in billions of US dollars (as of April 2021)

The Marvel Cinematic Universe franchise has grossed more than $22.5 billion worldwide—and counting! This impressive total includes ticket sales from the huge hits of 2018, *Black Panther* and *Avengers: Infinity War*. *Black Panther* grossed $1.34 billion worldwide within three months of its release, but then *Avengers: Infinity War* hit the screens, taking $1.82 billion worldwide in its first month. With *Avengers: Endgame* earning even greater revenues in 2019, and continued excitement for Marvel's upcoming Phase Four films in 2021 and beyond, the Marvel Cinematic Universe looks set to hold this record for the foreseeable future.

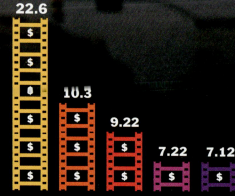

22.6 · 10.3 · 9.22 · 7.22 · 7.12

- Marvel Cinematic Universe
- Star Wars
- Harry Potter
- Spider-Man
- James Bond

first woman of color to win best director at the OSCARS

Chinese American filmmaker Chloé Zhao made Oscar history at the 2021 Academy Awards, becoming the first woman of color ever to win the best director award. Her film, *Nomadland*, tells the story of a middle-aged woman forced to live on the road after losing her home. The woman is played by Frances McDormand, who also won an Oscar for her performance. Zhao was born in Beijing, China, and lived in the UK before moving to the US permanently in her teens. Her success at this year's awards marks only the second time that a woman has won an Oscar for best director. The first woman to claim the prize was Kathryn Bigelow for her 2008 film, *The Hurt Locker*.

● Stage & Screen

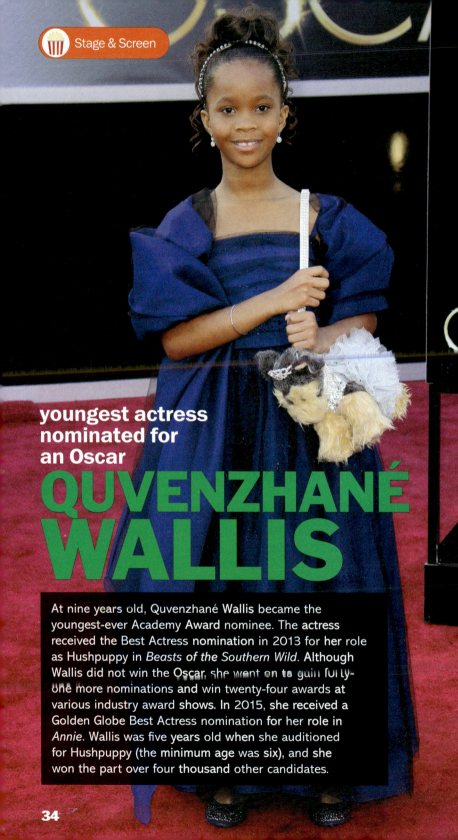

youngest actress nominated for an Oscar
QUVENZHANÉ WALLIS

At nine years old, Quvenzhané Wallis became the youngest-ever Academy Award nominee. The actress received the Best Actress nomination in 2013 for her role as Hushpuppy in *Beasts of the Southern Wild*. Although Wallis did not win the Oscar, she went on to gain forty-one more nominations and win twenty-four awards at various industry award shows. In 2015, she received a Golden Globe Best Actress nomination for her role in *Annie*. Wallis was five years old when she auditioned for Hushpuppy (the minimum age was six), and she won the part over four thousand other candidates.

youngest actor nominated for an Oscar
JUSTIN HENRY

Justin Henry was just seven years old when he received a Best Supporting Actor nomination for *Kramer vs. Kramer* in 1980. His neighbor, a casting director, suggested that Henry try out for the part. Although the young actor lost out on the Oscar, *Kramer vs. Kramer* won several Oscars, including Best Actor for Dustin Hoffman, Best Actress in a Supporting Role for Meryl Streep, and Best Picture. Justin Henry appeared in a few other films before leaving acting to finish his education. He then returned to acting in the 1990s.

 Stage & Screen

ACTRESSES WITH THE MOST MTV MOVIE AWARDS

 7 Jennifer Lawrence

 7 Kristen Stewart

 5 Shailene Woodley

 5 Sandra Bullock

 4 Alicia Silverstone

actresses with the most MTV Movie Awards
JENNIFER LAWRENCE
AND
KRISTEN STEWART

Jennifer Lawrence and Kristen Stewart share the title of actress with the most MTV Movie Awards for the fourth year running. Stewart won all seven of her awards for her role as Bella Swan in the movie adaptations of the *Twilight* franchise—including four Best Kiss awards with costar Robert Pattinson.

Lawrence's seventh award was for Best Hero, which she won in 2016 for her role as Katniss Everdeen in the fourth installment of the popular *Hunger Games* franchise. The actress, however, was a no-show at the awards ceremony that year, due to press commitments for her upcoming movie *X-Men: Apocalypse*.

ACTORS WITH THE MOST MTV MOVIE AWARDS

- **11** Jim Carrey
- **10** Robert Pattinson
- **7** Mike Myers
- **6** Adam Sandler
- **6** Will Smith

actor with the most MTV Movie Awards
JIM CARREY

Jim Carrey has eleven MTV Movie Awards, including five Best Comedic Performance awards for his roles in *Dumb and Dumber* (1994), *Ace Ventura: When Nature Calls* (1995), *The Cable Guy (1996)*, *Liar Liar* (1997), and *Yes Man* (2008). He won the Best Villain award twice, once for *The Cable Guy* (1996) and the second time for *Dr. Seuss' How the Grinch Stole Christmas* (2000). Fans also awarded Carrey with the Best Kiss award for his lip-lock with Lauren Holly in *Dumb and Dumber*.

Stage & Screen

top-earning actress
SOFÍA VERGARA

Small-screen superstar Sofía Vergara had it in the bag in 2020, surpassing her movie-star peers as the year's top-earning actress at $43 million. The year 2020 also marked nine years in a row of Vergara being the highest-paid actress on television, as she finished her role as Gloria Delgado-Pritchett on *Modern Family* and joined the judging panel of *America's Got Talent*. However, the business-savvy star doesn't earn her money only on camera; her lucrative moves include a line of jeans at Walmart, furniture at Rooms To Go, and her multimillion-dollar company, Latin World Entertainment.

TOP-EARNING ACTRESS OF 2020
In millions of US dollars

- $ Sofía Vergara
- $ Angelina Jolie
- $ Gal Gadot
- $ Melissa McCarthy
- $ Meryl Streep

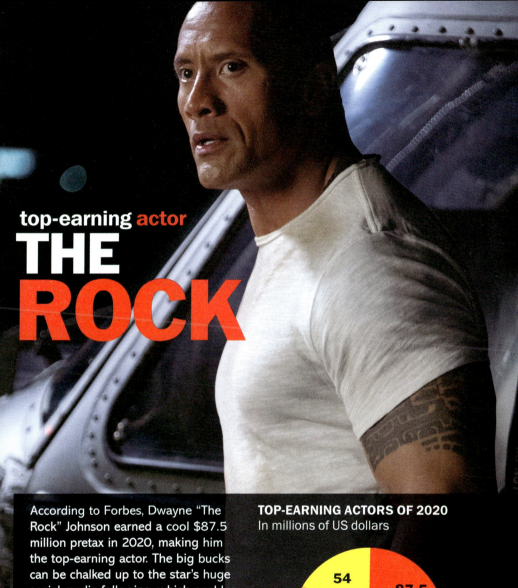

top-earning actor
THE ROCK

According to Forbes, Dwayne "The Rock" Johnson earned a cool $87.5 million pretax in 2020, making him the top-earning actor. The big bucks can be chalked up to the star's huge social media following, which enables financial deals outside of his acting career. Plus, he has clothing and shoe lines for Under Armour. Even with all the extra side businesses, the Rock earns most of his money from acting. Netflix paid him $23.5 million alone for his role in the action-thriller *Red Notice*, in which he stars alongside Ryan Reynolds and Gal Gadot.

TOP-EARNING ACTORS OF 2020
In millions of US dollars

- $ The Rock
- $ Ryan Reynolds
- $ Mark Wahlberg
- $ Ben Affleck
- $ Vin Diesel

Stage & Screen

top-grossing US movie
BAD BOYS FOR LIFE

The third installment in the *Bad Boys* franchise, *Bad Boys for Life*, was the highest-grossing film of 2020 for the US box office, making $204,417,855 in domestic sales. The follow-up to *Bad Boys* (1995) and *Bad Boys II* (2003), *Bad Boys for Life* stars Will Smith and Martin Lawrence as detectives investigating a series of murders. The movie was released on January 17, 2020, and earned $73.4 million over the four-day Martin Luther King Jr. holiday weekend, making it the biggest opening weekend of 2020—its January release occurring before COVID-19 became widespread in the United States. *Bad Boys for Life* was beaten only by the Chinese films *The Eight Hundred* and *My People, My Homeland* in the global box office, where it took in an impressive $424,536,881 in total.

top-grossing animated-film franchise
DESPICABLE ME

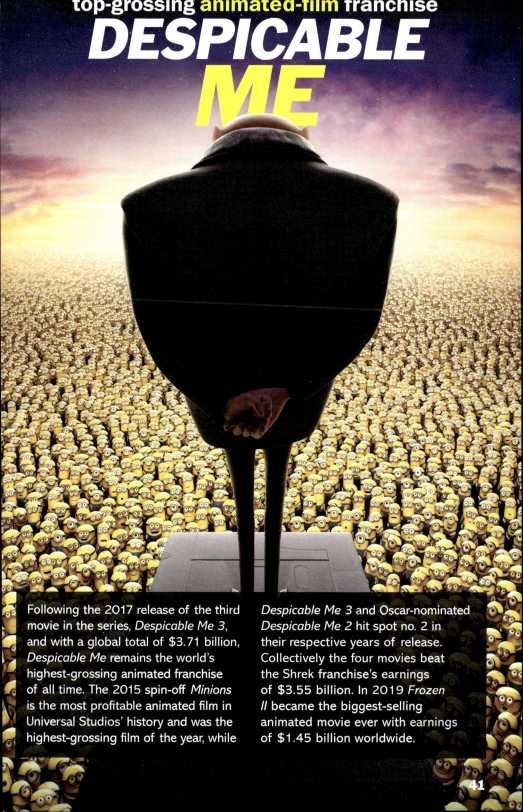

Following the 2017 release of the third movie in the series, *Despicable Me 3*, and with a global total of $3.71 billion, *Despicable Me* remains the world's highest-grossing animated franchise of all time. The 2015 spin-off *Minions* is the most profitable animated film in Universal Studios' history and was the highest-grossing film of the year, while *Despicable Me 3* and Oscar-nominated *Despicable Me 2* hit spot no. 2 in their respective years of release. Collectively the four movies beat the Shrek franchise's earnings of $3.55 billion. In 2019 *Frozen II* became the biggest-selling animated movie ever with earnings of $1.45 billion worldwide.

Stage & Screen

LONGEST-RUNNING BROADWAY SHOWS
Total performances (as of May 2020)

The Phantom of the Opera: **13,370**

Chicago (1996 revival): **9,692**

The Lion King: **9,302**

Cats: **7,485**

Les Misérables: **6,680**

longest-running Broadway show
THE PHANTOM OF THE OPERA

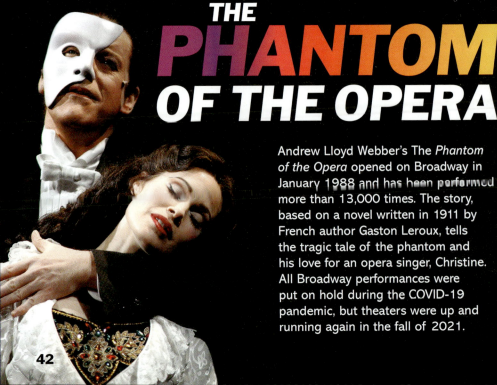

Andrew Lloyd Webber's The *Phantom of the Opera* opened on Broadway in January 1988 and has been performed more than 13,000 times. The story, based on a novel written in 1911 by French author Gaston Leroux, tells the tragic tale of the phantom and his love for an opera singer, Christine. All Broadway performances were put on hold during the COVID-19 pandemic, but theaters were up and running again in the fall of 2021.

highest-grossing Broadway musical
THE LION KING

Since opening on November 13, 1997, *The Lion King* has earned $1.7 billion. It's Broadway's third-longest-running production and is an adaptation of the hugely popular Disney animated film. Along with hit songs from the movie such as "Circle of Life" and "Hakuna Matata," the show includes new compositions by South African composer Lebo M. and others. The Broadway show features songs in six African languages, including Swahili and Congolese. Since it opened, *The Lion King* has attracted audiences totaling over one hundred million people.

Stage & Screen

musical with the most Tony Award nominations
HAMILTON

Lin-Manuel Miranda's musical biography of Founding Father Alexander Hamilton racked up sixteen Tony Award nominations to unseat the previous record holders, *The Producers* and *Billy Elliot: The Musical*, both of which had fifteen. The mega-hit hip-hop musical, which was inspired by historian Ron Chernow's biography of the first secretary of the treasury, portrays the Founding Fathers of the United States engaging in rap battles over issues such as the national debt and the French Revolution. *Hamilton* won eleven Tonys at the 2016 ceremony—one shy of *The Producers*, which retains the record for most Tony wins with twelve. *Hamilton's* Broadway success paved the way for the show to open in Chicago in 2016, with a touring show and a London production following in 2017.

youngest winner of a Laurence Olivier Award **ELEANOR WORTHINGTON-COX**
CLEO DEMETRIOU
KERRY INGRAM
SOPHIA KIELY

In 2012, four actresses shared an Olivier Award for their roles in the British production of *Matilda*. Eleanor Worthington-Cox, Cleo Demetriou, Kerry Ingram, and Sophia Kiely all won the award for Best Actress in a Musical. Of the four actresses, Worthington-Cox, age ten, was the youngest by a few weeks. Each actress portraying *Matilda* performs two shows a week. In the United States, the four *Matilda* actresses won a special Tony Honors for Excellence in the Theatre in 2013. *Matilda*, inspired by the book by Roald Dahl, won a record seven Olivier Awards in 2012.

ON THE MOVE

3

JUST LANDED
Perseverance reaches Mars

The fifth NASA rover to land on Mars touched down in February 2021, in what was the most complex landing ever attempted on the Red Planet. *Perseverance*, which was launched in June 2020, is on a mission to search Mars for signs of ancient life and to collect soil and rock samples in the hope that the rover might safely return to Earth with them. *Perseverance* is car-size: about 10 feet long, 9 feet wide, and 7 feet tall.

On the Move

trending

ROAD TO EQUALITY
Black Lives Matter Plaza

June 2020 saw cities across the United States declare their support for Black Lives Matter with giant murals painted onto the very streets where protestors had marched. In Washington, DC, seven artists painted 35-foot-tall yellow letters spelling out "Black Lives Matter" on Sixteenth Street directly in front of the White House. Honoring the movement, DC mayor Muriel Bowser promptly announced that this two-block section will now be known as Black Lives Matter Plaza.

A REAL GUNDAM SUIT?
Largest humanoid vehicle

A childhood dream came true for Japanese engineer Masaaki Nagumo in 2020, when the gigantic humanoid vehicle he designed was built by Japanese mechanical company Sakakibara Kikai. Named Mononofu, which means "samurai warrior" in Japanese, the robot holds a Guinness World Records title for the largest humanoid vehicle at 27 feet, 9 inches tall; 14 feet long; and 13 feet, 1 inch wide.

WHEELS UP
Longest bicycle wheelie

The longest distance traveled doing a continuous wheelie on a bicycle in one hour is now 19.23 miles (30.95 km). The new milestone was set by Swiss rider Manuel Scheidegger in September 2020, who completed more than seventy-seven laps of a 400-meter running track without his front wheel hitting the ground.

UP, UP, AND AWAY
Human spaceflight goes private

In May 2020, SpaceX sent up NASA astronauts Bob Behnken and Doug Hurley in their Crew Dragon spacecraft, marking the first human spaceflight launch by a private company. It was the first time in nine years that astronauts have been launched into space from the US! It was followed in November by SpaceX's first fully operational astronaut mission to the International Space Station, aboard the Crew Dragon craft Resilience.

49

🛪 On the Move

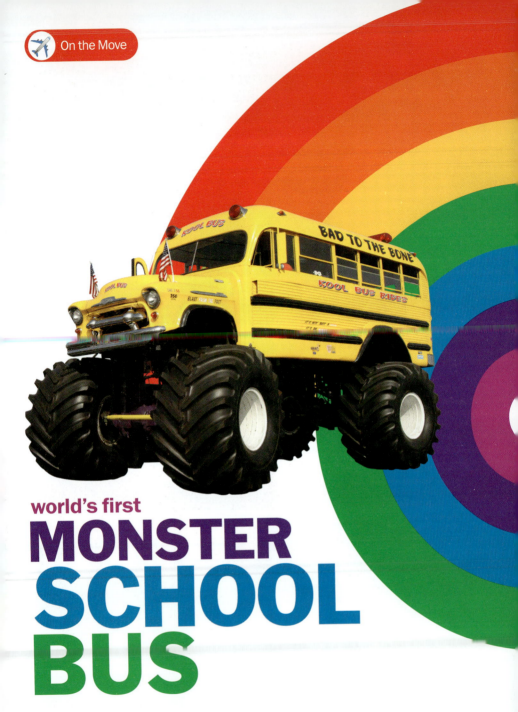

world's first
MONSTER SCHOOL BUS

"Bad to the Bone" was the first monster school bus in the world. This revamped 1956 yellow bus is 13 feet tall, thanks to massive tires with 25-inch rims. The oversize bus weighs 19,000 pounds and is a favorite ride at charity events in California. But don't expect to get anywhere in a hurry—this "Kool Bus" is not built for speed and goes at a maximum of just 7 miles per hour.

MOST EXPENSIVE CARS
In millions of US dollars

- Bugatti La Voiture Noire
- Pagani Zonda HP Barchetta
- Bugatti Centodieci
- Bugatti Divo
- Bugatti Chiron Super Sport 300+

most EXPENSIVE modern street-legal car
La Voiture Noire

In February 2019, La Voiture Noire (The Black Car) claimed the crown as the world's most expensive car after being sold for $12.5 million. Only one of these cars was produced by luxury French supercar-maker Bugatti, in celebration of its 110th anniversary. Said to take inspiration from the manufacturer's Type 57 SC Atlantic of the 1930s, as well as Darth Vader from *Star Wars*, the car features a sleek, all-black design with six tailpipes. Now worth an estimated $18.7 million, this exclusive vehicle can hit 261 miles per hour at top speed and can reach 62 miles per hour in 2.4 seconds.

On the Move

SIN CITY HUSTLER
world's longest monster truck

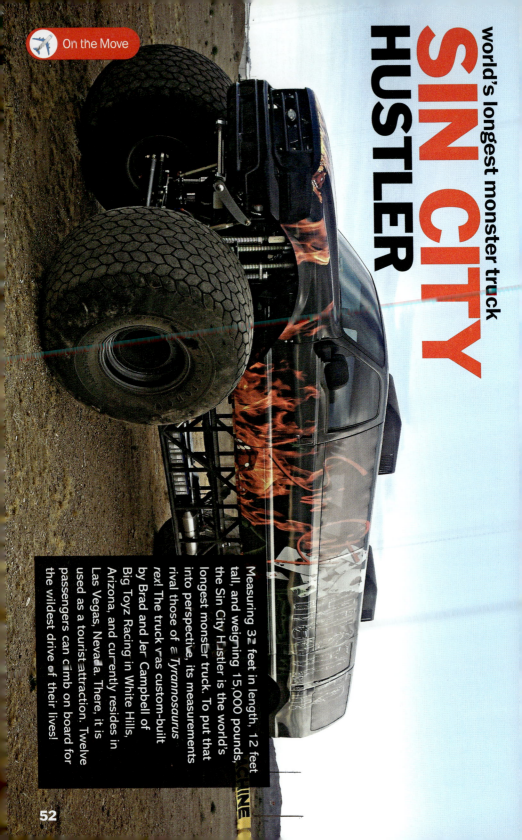

Measuring 32 feet in length, 12 feet tall, and weighing 15,000 pounds, the Sin City Hustler is the world's longest monster truck. To put that into perspective, its measurements rival those of a *Tyrannosaurus rex*! The truck was custom-built by Brad and Jen Campbell of Big Toyz Racing in White Hills, Arizona, and currently resides in Las Vegas, Nevada. There, it is used as a tourist attraction. Twelve passengers can climb on board for the wildest drive of their lives!

world's smallest trailer
QTVAN

The tiny QTvan is just over 7 feet long, 2.5 feet wide, and 5 feet tall. Inside, however, it has a full-size single bed, a kettle for boiling water, and a 19-inch TV. The Environmental Transport Association (ETA) in Britain sponsored the invention of the minitrailer, which was designed to be pulled by a mobility scooter. The ETA recommends the QTvan for short trips only, since mobility scooters have a top speed of 6 miles per hour, at best.

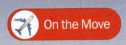

On the Move

fastest land vehicle
THRUST SSC

The world's fastest car is the Thrust SSC, which reached a speed of 763 miles per hour on October 15, 1997, in the Black Rock Desert of Nevada. *SSC* stands for supersonic (faster than the speed of sound). The Thrust SSC's amazing speed comes from two jet engines with 110,000 brake horsepower. That's as much as 145 Formula One race cars. The British-made car uses about 5 gallons of jet fuel in one second and takes just five seconds to reach its top speed. At that speed, the Thrust SSC could travel from New York City to San Francisco in less than four hours. More recently, another British manufacturer has developed a new supersonic car, the Bloodhound, with a projected speed of 1,000 miles per hour. If it reaches that, it will set a new world record.

fastest passenger train
SHANGHAI MAGLEV

The Shanghai Maglev, which runs between Shanghai Pudong International Airport and the outskirts of Shanghai, is currently the fastest passenger train in the world. The service reaches speeds of 268 miles per hour, covering the 19-mile distance in seven minutes and twenty seconds. *Maglev* is short for magnetic levitation, as the train moves by floating on magnets rather than with wheels on a track. Other high-speed trains, such as Japan's SCMaglev, may have reached higher speeds in testing (375 miles per hour), but are capped at 200 miles per hour when carrying passengers.

FASTEST PASSENGER TRAINS
(maximum operating speed)

Shanghai Maglev: **268 mph**
China Harmony: **236 mph**
Italy Italo: **224 mph**
Spain Velaro: **217 mph**
Spain Talgo 350: **217 mph**

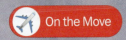
On the Move

X-43A
fastest unpiloted plane

In November 2004, NASA launched its experimental X-43A plane for a test flight over the Pacific Ocean. The X-43A plane reached Mach 9.6, which is more than nine times the speed of sound and nearly 7,000 miles per hour. A B-52 aircraft carried the X-43A and a Pegasus rocket booster into the air, releasing them at 40,000 feet. At that point, the booster—essentially a fuel-packed engine—ignited, blasting the unpiloted X-43A higher and faster, before separating from the plane. The plane continued to fly for several minutes at 110,000 feet, before crashing (intentionally) into the ocean.

56

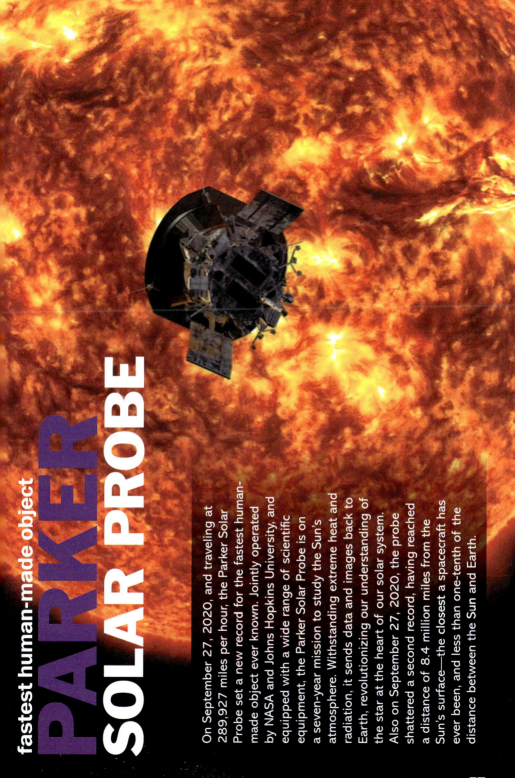

fastest human-made object
PARKER SOLAR PROBE

On September 27, 2020, and traveling at 289,927 miles per hour, the Parker Solar Probe set a new record for the fastest human-made object ever known. Jointly operated by NASA and Johns Hopkins University, and equipped with a wide range of scientific equipment, the Parker Solar Probe is on a seven-year mission to study the Sun's atmosphere. Withstanding extreme heat and radiation, it sends data and images back to Earth, revolutionizing our understanding of the star at the heart of our solar system. Also on September 27, 2020, the probe shattered a second record, having reached a distance of 8.4 million miles from the Sun's surface—the closest a spacecraft has ever been, and less than one-tenth of the distance between the Sun and Earth.

✈ On the Move

APOLLO 10 FLIGHT STATS

05/18/69
LAUNCH DATE: May 18, 1969

12:49
LAUNCH TIME: 12:49 p.m. EDT

05/21/69
ENTERED LUNAR ORBIT: May 21, 1969

192:03:23
DURATION OF MISSION: 192 hours, 3 minutes, 23 seconds

05/26/69
RETURN DATE: May 26, 1969

12:52
SPLASHDOWN: 12:52 p.m. EDT

LIFT-OFF
The Apollo 10 spacecraft was launched from Cape Canaveral, known as Cape Kennedy at the time. It was the fourth crewed Apollo launch in seven months.

fastest crewed

SPACECRAFT
APOLLO 10

NASA's Apollo 10 spacecraft reached its top speed on its descent to Earth, hurtling through the atmosphere at 24,816 miles per hour and splashing down on May 26, 1969. The spacecraft's crew had traveled faster than anyone on Earth. The mission was a "dress rehearsal" for the first moon landing by Apollo 11, two months later. The Apollo 10 spacecraft consisted of a Command and Service Module, called Charlie Brown, and a Lunar Module, called Snoopy. Today, Charlie Brown is on display at the Science Museum in London, England.

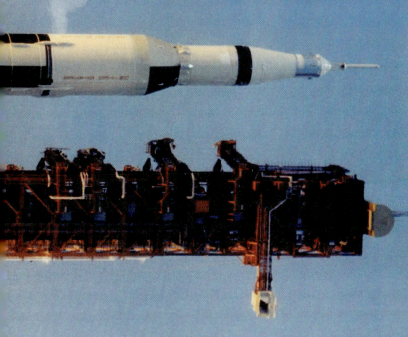

 **On the Move**

fastest roller coaster
FORMULA ROSSA

FORMULA ROSSA
World Records
Speed: 149.1 mph
G-force: 1.7 Gs
Acceleration: 4.8 Gs

Thrill seekers hurtle along the Formula Rossa track at 149.1 miles per hour. The high-speed roller coaster is part of Ferrari World in Abu Dhabi, United Arab Emirates. Ferrari World also features the world's largest indoor theme park, at 1.5 million square feet. The Formula Rossa roller coaster seats are red Ferrari-shaped cars that travel from 0 to 62 miles per hour in just two seconds—as fast as a race car. The ride's G-force is so extreme that passengers must wear goggles to protect their eyes. G-force acts on a body due to acceleration and gravity. People can withstand 6 to 8 Gs for short periods. The Formula Rossa G-force is 4.8 Gs during acceleration and 1.7 Gs at maximum speed.

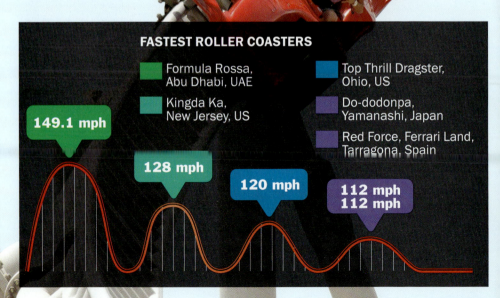

FASTEST ROLLER COASTERS

- Formula Rossa, Abu Dhabi, UAE — 149.1 mph
- Kingda Ka, New Jersey, US — 128 mph
- Top Thrill Dragster, Ohio, US — 120 mph
- Do-dodonpa, Yamanashi, Japan — 112 mph
- Red Force, Ferrari Land, Tarragona, Spain — 112 mph

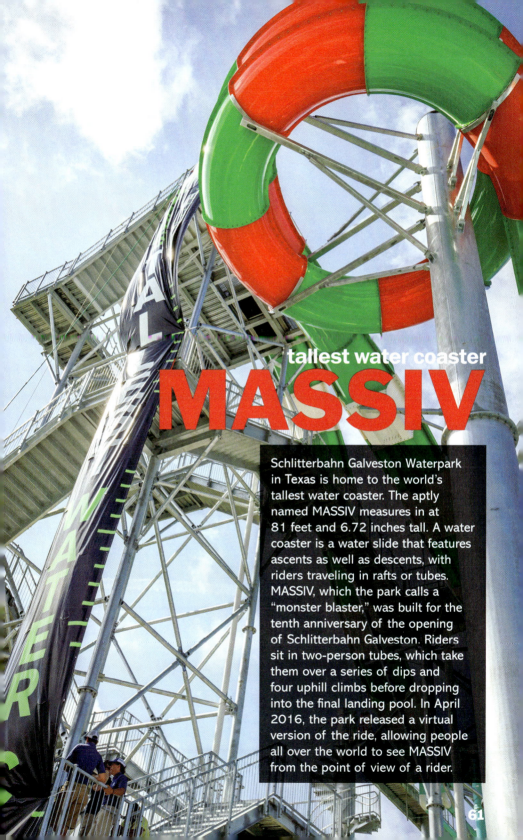

tallest water coaster
MASSIV

Schlitterbahn Galveston Waterpark in Texas is home to the world's tallest water coaster. The aptly named MASSIV measures in at 81 feet and 6.72 inches tall. A water coaster is a water slide that features ascents as well as descents, with riders traveling in rafts or tubes. MASSIV, which the park calls a "monster blaster," was built for the tenth anniversary of the opening of Schlitterbahn Galveston. Riders sit in two-person tubes, which take them over a series of dips and four uphill climbs before dropping into the final landing pool. In April 2016, the park released a virtual version of the ride, allowing people all over the world to see MASSIV from the point of view of a rider.

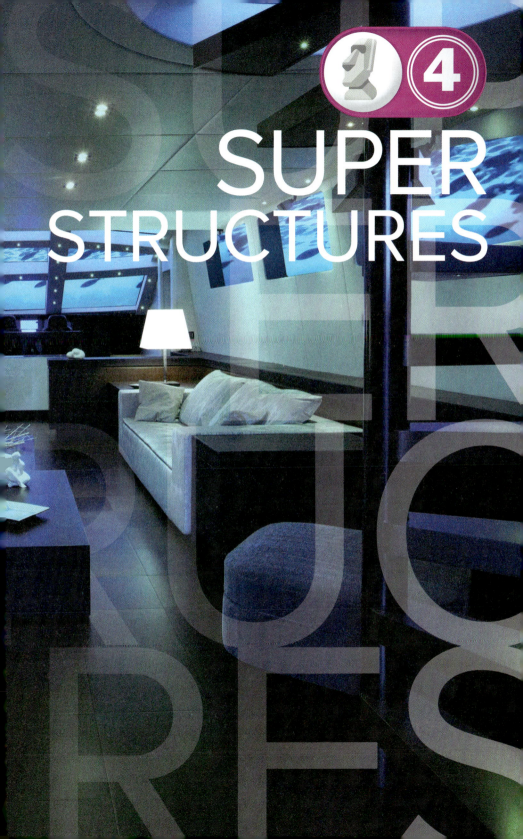

SUPER STRUCTURES

4

ECO-INGENUITY
Largest urban rooftop greenhouse

A 163,800-square-foot greenhouse now exists in Ville Saint-Laurent, Montreal . . . on top of an old warehouse! The newest Lufa Farms project, completed in August 2020, is big enough to grow food for 10,000 families. Lufa Farms has three other rooftop greenhouses, but the Ville Saint-Laurent farm is bigger than the other three combined. All four projects are helping to bring local, sustainable agriculture into the big city.

COCOA-VILLE
Town dusted with cocoa powder

Locals in the Swiss town of Olten stepped outside in August 2020 to find it raining cocoa powder! The fairy-tale "storm" was apparently the result of a small defect in the ventilation system at the town's Lindt & Sprüngli chocolate factory, leading to dust from cacao nibs to be distributed by some strong winds. It left a small area of the town covered in a fine spread of chocolaty dust.

PUT TO GOOD (RE-)USE
From discarded PPE to bricks

The COVID-19 pandemic produced huge numbers of disposable face masks, many of them made from polypropylene plastic, which takes a very long time to degrade. Indian eco-activist Binish Desai found a constructive way to recycle them, by turning discarded PPE into bricks for construction. By the end of 2020, the twenty-seven-year-old had created at least 40,000 of these bricks, with plans to make 15,000 of them a day going into 2021.

SHATTERED HOPES
Iconic telescope is destroyed

Several unhappy events in 2020 led to the destruction of Puerto Rico's Arecibo Observatory, containing what was at the time the world's second-largest single-dish radio telescope. The telescope had already been decommissioned by the time its 900-ton equipment platform fell 450 feet in December, shattering most of the telescope and its dish. The telescope will be remembered for its achievements in tracking asteroids, and for being the site of a message sent out searching for extraterrestrial life in 1974.

WHALE TAIL TO THE RESCUE
Metro train's lucky catch

An art sculpture made a surprising safety net in November 2020, when a Dutch metro train crashed through a safety barrier and seemed to be headed for a disastrous fall. The train was saved from the 32-foot drop into water by a large art installation of a whale tail, which caught the train and held it suspended in the air. The train was empty except for its driver, who escaped injury. In a funny coincidence, the plastic art piece, installed in 2002, is named *Saved by the Whale's Tail*.

 Super Structures

trending

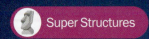 Super Structures

city with the most skyscrapers in the world
HONG KONG

CITIES WITH THE MOST SKYSCRAPERS IN THE WORLD
Number of skyscrapers at 500 feet or higher

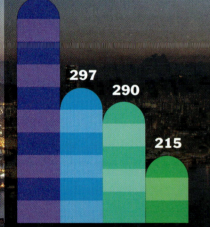

- 482 Hong Kong, China
- 297 Shenzhen, China
- 290 New York City, US
- 215 Dubai, UAE

Hong Kong, China, has 482 buildings that reach 500 feet or higher, and twenty-six under construction. Six are 1,000 feet or higher. The tallest three are the International Commerce Centre (ICC) at 1,588 feet; Two International Finance Centre at 1,352 feet; and Central Plaza at 1,227 feet. Hong Kong's stunning skyline towers above Victoria Harbour. Most of its tallest buildings are on Hong Kong Island, although the other side of the harbor, Kowloon, is growing. Every night a light, laser, and sound show called "A Symphony of Lights" illuminates the sky against a backdrop of about forty of Hong Kong's skyscrapers.

world's largest sports stadium
RUNGRADO 1ST OF MAY STADIUM

It took over two years to build Rungrado 1st of May Stadium, a huge sports venue that seats up to 114,000 people. The 197-foot-tall stadium opened in 1989 on Rungra Island in North Korea's capital, Pyongyang. The stadium hosts international soccer matches on its natural grass pitch and has other facilities such as an indoor swimming pool, training halls, and a 1,312-foot rubberized running track. A newcomer to the list, the second-largest venue, India's Narendra Modi Stadium, was inaugurated in 2020.

LARGEST SPORTS STADIUMS
By capacity

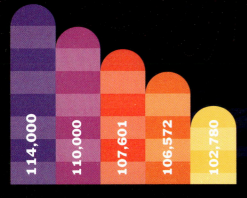

- Rungrado 1st of May Stadium, North Korea
- Narendra Modi Stadium, Ahmedabad, India
- Michigan Stadium, Michigan, US
- Beaver Stadium, Pennsylvania, US
- Ohio Stadium, Ohio, US

114,000 | 110,000 | 107,601 | 106,572 | 102,780

67

Super Structures

LOVER'S DEEP

world's most expensive hotel

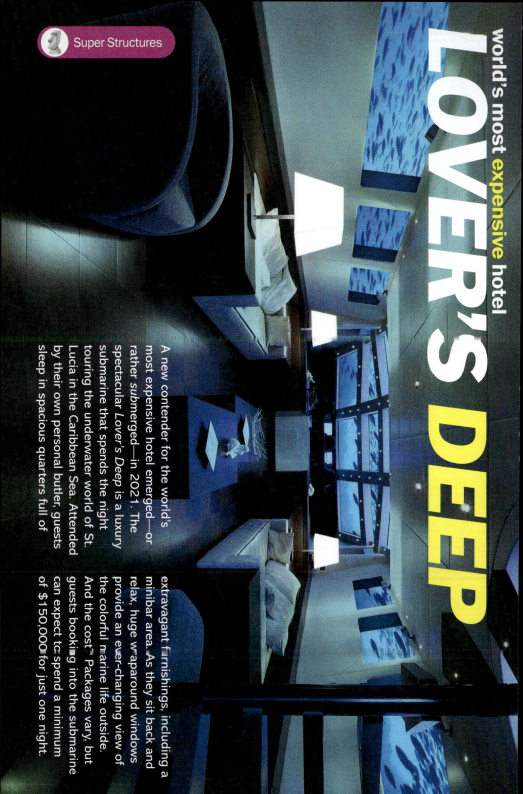

A new contender for the world's most expensive hotel emerged—or rather *submerged*—in 2021. The spectacular *Lover's Deep* is a luxury submarine that spends the night touring the underwater world of St. Lucia in the Caribbean Sea. Attended by their own personal butler, guests sleep in spacious quarters full of extravagant furnishings, including a minibar area. As they sit back and relax, huge wraparound windows provide an ever-changing view of the colorful marine life outside. And the cost? Packages vary, but guests booking into the submarine can expect to spend a minimum of $150,000 for just one night.

PALACIO DE SAL

world's first hotel made of salt

Hotel Palacio de Sal in Uyuni, Bolivia, is the first hotel in the world made completely out of salt. Originally built in 1998, construction began on the new Palacio de Sal in 2004. The hotel overlooks the biggest salt flat in the world, Salar de Uyuni, which covers 4,086 square miles. Builders used around one million blocks of salt to create the hotel walls, floors, ceilings, and furniture. Some of the hotel's thirty rooms have igloo-shaped roofs. The salt flats lie in an area once covered by Lago Minchin, an ancient salt lake. When the lake dried up, it left salt pans, one of which was the Salar de Uyuni.

ANOTHER STRANGE PLACE TO STAY

Hotel shaped like a dog: Dog Bark Park Inn in Cottonwood, Idaho, where you can sleep inside a wooden beagle that measures 33 feet tall and 16 feet wide.

Super Structures

DUBAI'S BURJ KHALIFA WORLD RECORDS:
Tallest building: **2,717** feet
Most floors: **163**
Highest restaurant: **1,448** feet from ground level

Laid end to end, the steel used here would

world's
tallest
building

BURJ
KHALIFA

stretch one-quarter of the way around the world!

GOING
UP!

The upper section is steel framed, so it's possible to make it taller. During building, its height was raised three times.

 Super Structures

world's largest freestanding building
NEW CENTURY GLOBAL CENTER

The New Century Global Center in Chengdu, southwestern China, is an enormous 18.9 million square feet. That's nearly three times the size of the Pentagon, in Arlington, Virginia. Completed in 2013, the structure is 328 feet tall, 1,640 feet long, and 1,312 feet deep. The multiuse building houses a 4.3-million-square-foot shopping mall, two hotels, an Olympic-size ice rink, a fourteen-screen IMAX cinema complex, and offices. It even has its own **Paradise** Island, a beach resort complete with artificial sun.

world's largest swimming pool
CITYSTARS POOL

Citystars Sharm el-Sheikh lagoon, in Egypt, stretches over 30 acres. It was created by Crystal Lagoons, the same company that built the former record holder at San Alfonso del Mar in Chile. The lagoon at Sharm el-Sheikh cost $5.5 million to create and is designed to be sustainable, using salt water from local underground aquifers. The creators purify this water not just for recreation, but also to provide clean, fresh water to the surrounding community.

LARGEST SWIMMING POOLS
Size in acres

- Citystars, Sharm el-Sheikh, Egypt
- San Alfonso del Mar, Algarrobo, Chile
- MahaSamutr, Hua Hin, Thailand
- Dreamworld Fun Lagoon, Karachi, Pakistan
- Piscine Alfred Nakache, Toulouse, France

Super Structures

world's longest bridge
DANYANG-KUNSHAN GRAND BRIDGE

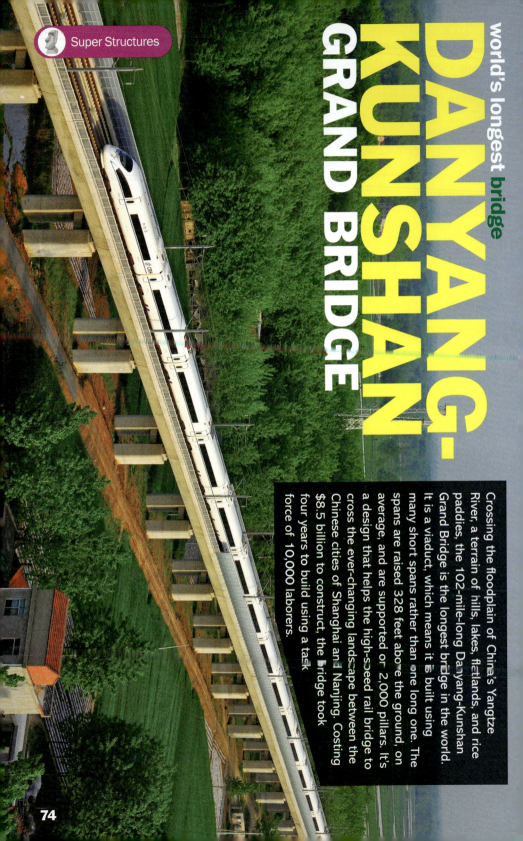

Crossing the floodplain of China's Yangtze River, a terrain of hills, lakes, fletlands, and rice paddies, the 102-mile-long Danyang-Kunshan Grand Bridge is the longest bridge in the world. It is a viaduct, which means it is built using many short spans rather than one long one. The spans are raised 328 feet above the ground, on average, and are supported on 2,000 pillars. It's a design that helps the high-speed rail bridge to cross the ever-changing landscape between the Chinese cities of Shanghai and Nanjing. Costing $8.5 billion to construct, the bridge took four years to build using a task force of 10,000 laborers.

world's greenest city
TAMPA

According to the Senseable City Laboratory at Massachusetts Institute of Technology (MIT), Tampa, Florida, currently has the highest percentage of urban greenery among the thirty cities in its ongoing Treepedia study. By analyzing panoramas posted on Google Street View, the program assesses the level of vegetation in a city and rates it on a scale of 0–100 in its Green View Index (GVI). It shows the real level of greenery in the streets on which city people live and work. The people behind Treepedia hope to raise greater awareness in cities where trees are lacking and to encourage developers to include them in future projects.

GREENEST CITIES
Treepedia's GVI rating

- Tampa, Florida — 36.1%
- Breda, the Netherlands — 29.3%
- Singapore — 28.8%
- Oslo, Norway — 25.9%
- Sydney, Australia — 25.6%
- Vancouver, Canada — 25.3%

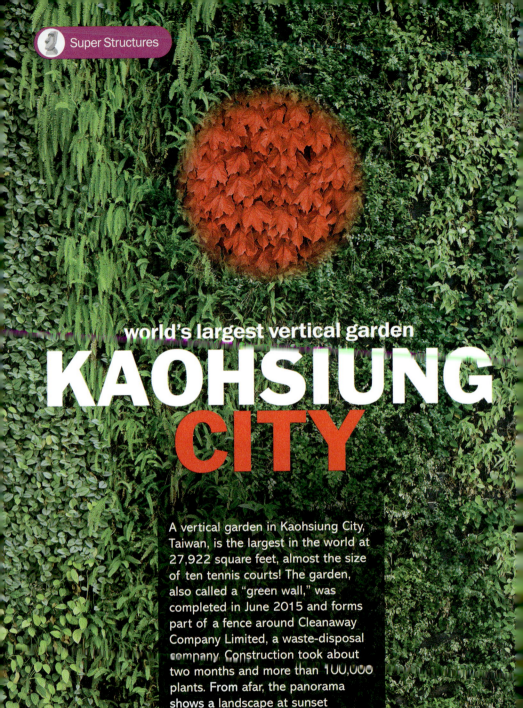

Super Structures

world's largest vertical garden

KAOHSIUNG CITY

A vertical garden in Kaohsiung City, Taiwan, is the largest in the world at 27,922 square feet, almost the size of ten tennis courts! The garden, also called a "green wall," was completed in June 2015 and forms part of a fence around Cleanaway Company Limited, a waste-disposal company. Construction took about two months and more than 100,000 plants. From afar, the panorama shows a landscape at sunset with a bright red sun. However, green walls are not only beautiful; they help to lower pollution and carbon-dioxide emissions.

COUNTRY WITH THE MOST GREENHOUSES

The Netherlands: Greenhouses cover more than 36 square miles of the country's entire area.

world's largest greenhouse
EDEN PROJECT

The Eden Project sprawls over 32 acres of land in the countryside of Cornwall, England. Nestled in the cavity of a china clay pit, it's the world's largest greenhouse and has been open since 2003. Eight interlinked, transparent domes house two distinct biomes. The first is a rain forest region and the second is Mediterranean. Each has around one thousand plant varieties. Visitors can see a further three thousand different plants in the 20 acres of outdoor gardens. During construction, the Eden Project used a record-breaking 230 miles of scaffolding.

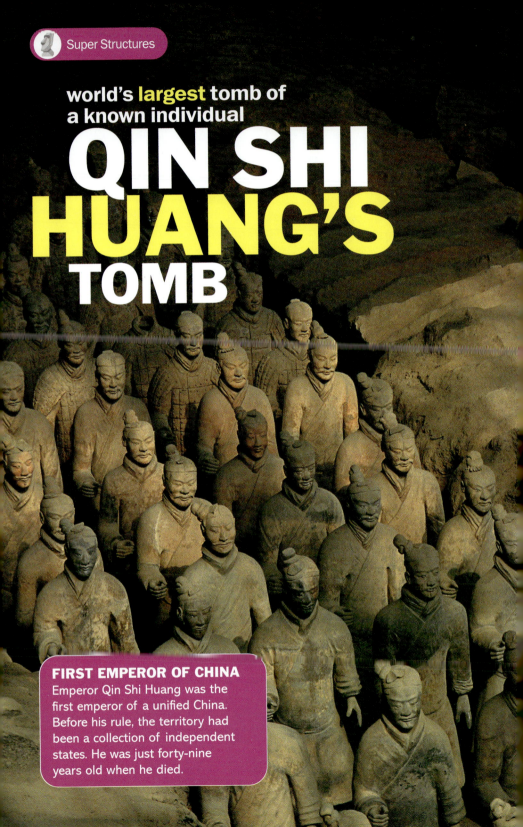

Super Structures

world's **largest** tomb of a known individual

QIN SHI HUANG'S TOMB

FIRST EMPEROR OF CHINA
Emperor Qin Shi Huang was the first emperor of a unified China. Before his rule, the territory had been a collection of independent states. He was just forty-nine years old when he died.

QIN SHI HUANG'S TOMB STATS

1974 YEAR of discovery

36 NUMBER of years to create

8,000 TOTAL NUMBER of figures found

221–207 DURATION of the Ion Dynasty, BCE

Emperor Qin Shi Huang ruled China from 221 to 207 BCE. In 1974, people digging a well in the fields northeast of Xi'an, in the Shaanxi province, accidentally discovered the ancient tomb. Further investigation revealed a burial complex over 20 square miles. A large pit contained 6,000 life-size, terra-cotta warrior figures, each one different from the next and dressed according to rank.

A second and third pit contained 2,000 more figures, clay horses, about 40,000 bronze weapons, and other artifacts. Historians think that 700,000 people worked for about thirty-six years to create this incredible mausoleum. The emperor's tomb remains sealed to preserve its contents and to protect workers from possible hazards, such as chemical poisoning from mercury in the surrounding soil.

Super Structures

world's largest castle
PRAGUE CASTLE

Founded in the late ninth century, Prague Castle is officially the largest coherent castle complex in the world. Covering an area of 750,000 square feet, the castle grounds span enough land for seven football fields, with buildings in various architectural styles that have been added and renovated during past centuries. Formerly the home of kings and emperors, the castle is now occupied by the president of the Czech Republic and his family and is also open to tourists. The palace contains four churches, including the famous St. Vitus Cathedral.

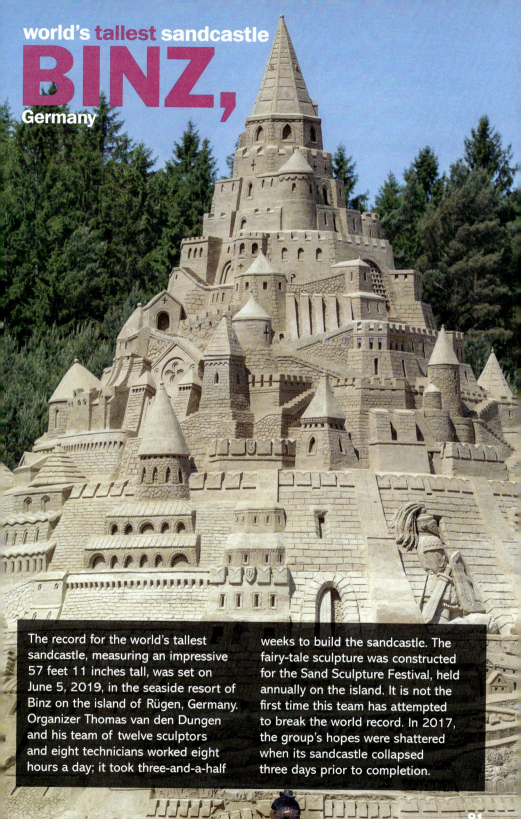

world's tallest sandcastle
BINZ,
Germany

The record for the world's tallest sandcastle, measuring an impressive 57 feet 11 inches tall, was set on June 5, 2019, in the seaside resort of Binz on the island of Rügen, Germany. Organizer Thomas van den Dungen and his team of twelve sculptors and eight technicians worked eight hours a day; it took three-and-a-half weeks to build the sandcastle. The fairy-tale sculpture was constructed for the Sand Sculpture Festival, held annually on the island. It is not the first time this team has attempted to break the world record. In 2017, the group's hopes were shattered when its sandcastle collapsed three days prior to completion.

Super Structures

world's longest LEGO® ship
WORLD DREAM

In 2018, 1,000 cruise passengers and volunteers came together to help build a replica of the *World Dream* cruise ship, a vessel owned by China's Dream Cruises Management Ltd. Boasting more than 2.5 million LEGO® blocks, this spectacle is the longest LEGO® ship ever built. It's a completely scaled down replica of the *World Dream* cruise ship, with all eighteen of its decks, and measures 27 feet, 8.5 inches in length. On completion it was placed in Hong Kong's Kai Tak Cruise Terminal for all to see.

world's largest sculpture
cut from a single piece of stone
SPHINX

The Great Sphinx stands guard near three large pyramids in Giza, Egypt. Historians believe ancient people created the sculpture about 4,500 years ago for the pharaoh Khafre. They carved the sphinx from one mass of limestone in the desert floor, creating a sculpture about 66 feet high and 240 feet long. It has the head of a pharaoh and the body of a lion. The sculpture may represent Ruti, a twin lion god from ancient myths that protected the sun god, Ra, and guarded entrances to the underworld. Sand has covered and preserved the Great Sphinx, but over many years, wind and humidity have worn parts of the soft limestone away, some of which have been restored using blocks of sand and quicklime.

GREAT SPHINX FACTS
Age: 4,500 years (estimated)
Length: 240 feet
Height: 66 feet

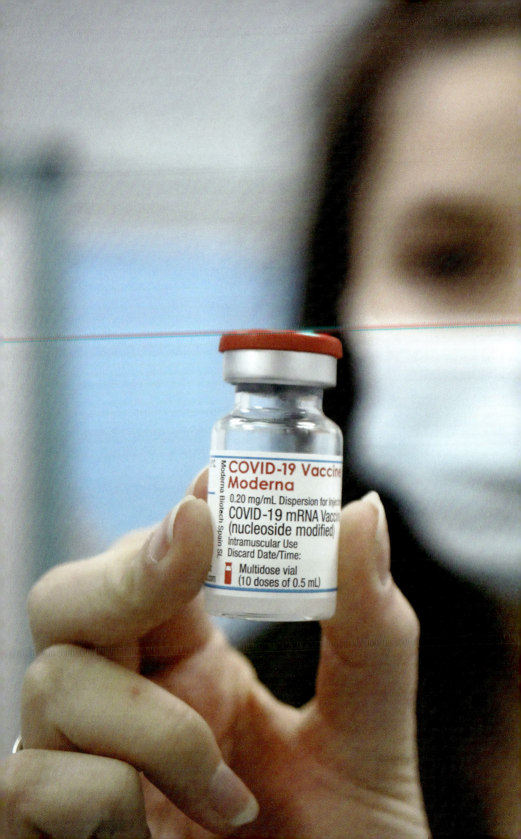

HIGH TECH

5

trending

High Tech

MECHA-MONSTERS
Robotic wolves scare off bears

The Japanese town of Takikawa came up with a particularly innovative solution to its bear problem in 2020: robotic wolves! After sightings of wild bears roaming the town's streets, the town decided to install two "robot monster wolves"—animatronic red-eyed robots fitted with motion sensors, which move their heads and growl through speakers to scare off the roving bears without hurting them. So far, so good: no bears have been spotted in Takikawa since then!

Many of those hoping to bag a PlayStation 5 in 2021 were disappointed, as Sony failed to meet demands for its new console. Launched in November 2020, the PS5 swiftly became the fastest-selling console ever, but the tech giant simply could not produce enough units. A major reason for falling short was a global shortage of essential components caused by the COVID-19 pandemic. And the future doesn't look much better. In May 2021, Sony hinted that shortages could continue long into 2022.

NOW YOU SEE IT...
PS5: Fastest-selling console

THE SILVER LINING
Video comms get a boost

Video technology was a saving grace during the COVID-19 pandemic, which made Zoom a household name. The software, which allows videoconferences with multiple participants, was used by both companies and individuals alike, leading to a huge boost in Zoom's revenue—in August, they revealed that revenue had gone up 355 percent from previous years. The word "Zoom" itself became a verb in 2020, meaning to talk to people via video call.

Followers of SpaceX founder Elon Musk and Canadian musician Grimes had a lot of questions in May 2020, when the couple announced the arrival of their baby X Æ A-12 Musk (pronounced "X Ash Archangel"). According to Grimes, X represents an "unknown variable," Æ is an "Elven spelling of AI," and the A-12 is an airplane known as the Archangel. The parents later changed the name to X Æ A-Xii due to California's laws against using nonalphabetical characters in names.

HAPPY BIRTHDAY TO . . .
Unusual baby name goes viral

FACT CHECK!
Twitter takes on fake news

Social media giant Twitter took a stand against misinformation in 2020, when it began adding disclaimers to tweets containing misleading information—even those made by elected officials! In May, Twitter announced that it would be adding labels for disputed, misleading, or unverified information, especially targeting tweets with harmful misinformation about COVID-19. Later in the year, these labels were also applied to tweets that emerged during the US presidential election.

High Tech

celebrity with the most Instagram followers
CRISTIANO RONALDO

Portuguese soccer icon Cristiano Ronaldo was once again the year's most followed celebrity on Instagram in 2021. He now has 271 million followers, an increase of 45 million over last year. His post in remembrance of Argentine football legend Diego Maradona, who died in November 2020, is the third-most liked Instagram of all time. Ronaldo is the forward for Juventus and the captain of the national Portuguese team. The only other soccer player to make the top-ten list for most Instagram followers is Lionel Messi in the no. 8 spot with 191m followers.

CELEBRITIES WITH THE MOST INSTAGRAM FOLLOWERS
In millions of followers (as of February 2021)

 Cristiano Ronaldo
271

 Ariana Grande
227

 The Rock
224

 Kylie Jenner
222

 Selena Gomez
217

88

YUSAKU MAEZAWA

most retweeted tweet ever

🔁 4.4m   ↑ Share this Tweet

Yusaku Maezawa holds the title for the most retweeted tweet of all time, with a whopping 4.4 million retweets. Celebrating his company's high Christmas–New Year earnings in 2018–2019, the Japanese billionaire posted a tweet with accompanying images promising to split one hundred million yen ($937,638) among one hundred randomly chosen people. Another giveaway from Yusaku (who tweets as @yousuck2020) also made the list as the second-most retweeted tweet. The prospect of free money definitely helped motivate people to make this one go viral!

High Tech

TOP-GROSSING IPHONE GAMING APPS
Daily revenue in US dollars (as of October 2020)

Game	Revenue
Roblox	2,511,808
Call of Duty Mobile	2,511,808
Pokémon GO	1,941,308
Candy Crush Saga	1,883,069
Clash of Clans	1,488,789

ROBLOX/ CALL OF DUTY
highest-grossing iPhone gaming apps

Roblox was once again the highest-grossing iPhone game app at the end of 2020, but this year it shared the top spot with *Call of Duty*'s mobile version, released in October 2019. Both apps had around $2.5 million in daily revenue in October 2020. *Call of Duty: Mobile* is the franchise's first free-to-play mobile version, and had more than 300 million downloads as of November 2020—many of which clearly led users to purchase in-app extras. Previous joint leader *Candy Crush*, also owned by *Call of Duty*'s parent company Activision, fell to fourth in the all-time chart in 2020, grossing around $1,883,070 per day.

90

most-viewed YouTube video ever "BABY SHARK DANCE"

Half of the top 10 most-viewed YouTube videos now are specifically for entertaining children, and the no. 1 spot is no exception. The addictive "Baby Shark Dance" video by South Korean brand Pinkfong (by SmartStudy) has been viewed at least 8.3 billion times since its upload in June 2016. The simple song and its accompanying dance moves went viral in 2018, and "Baby Shark Dance" now has its own line of merchandise as well as an animated series on Nickelodeon. There is even a remix starring Luis Fonsi, which is ironic, given that Fonsi's "Despacito" was no. 1 prior to "Baby Shark Dance."

91

High Tech

most-used
INSTAGRAM HASHTAG

The most popular hashtag on Instagram in 2020 was used to caption a variety of photographs—romantic selfies, cute animals, and shots of favorite foods. The picture-sharing platform displays 1.82 billion posts that use the tag #love. Taking second spot on the listings in 2020 with 1.14 billion posts was #instagood, for photos that are just "too good" not to share. Also rising in the ranks are, #fashion, #photooftheday, #beautiful, and #art

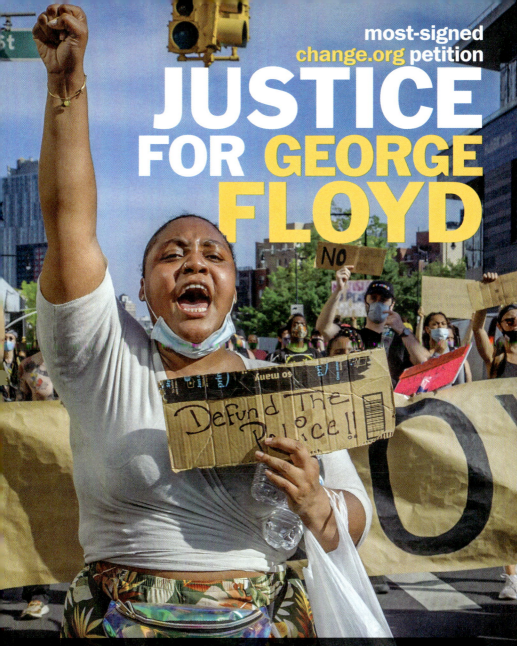

most-signed change.org petition

JUSTICE FOR GEORGE FLOYD

In June 2020, "Justice for George Floyd" became change.org's most-signed petition ever, with eighteen million signatures. The petition called for the four police officers involved in Floyd's death to be fired and arrested. George Floyd, a Black man, died on May 25 after White officer Derek Chauvin knelt on his neck for almost nine minutes during an arrest, with three fellow officers standing by. Video footage of the event went viral, sparking anti-racism protests across the globe. In April 2021, Derek Chauvin was found guilty of three charges of killing George Floyd.

High Tech

most-viewed video on TikTok
ZACH KING

Proving that the world still loves watching magic, four of the five most-viewed videos on the TikTok platform as of January 2021 come from American illusionist Zach King. The most popular TikTok video ever, with 2.2 billion views, shows King pulling off a Harry Potter-based trick in which he uses a longboard and mirrored surface to create the illusion of flying on a broomstick down a Californian street. The only TikTok in the top five that is not by King comes from makeup YouTuber James Charles, whose "Sisters Christmas Party" 2019 TikTok became the app's second-most viewed ever with 1.7 billion views.

first account to reach 100m on TikTok
CHARLI D'AMELIO

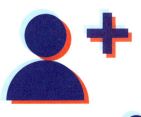

Sixteen-year-old influencer Charli D'Amelio became the first TikTok user to hit one hundred million followers on the app in November 2020. The social media personality, who joined the app in 2019, quickly became known for her lip-syncing and dancing challenge videos. Her one hundred million milestone came at a controversial time, with D'Amelio losing around one million followers for her behavior in a "Dinner with the D'Amelios" YouTube segment. Despite this, D'Amelio's online presence has earned her an estimated net worth of $8 million, including income from movie roles and brand partnerships.

High Tech

10.4M

dog with the most Instagram followers
JIFFPOM

On May 3, 2017, and with 4.8 million followers, Jiffpom broke the Guinness World Record for being the most popular dog on Instagram. Three years later, in June 2020, the dog's follower count was at the 10.4-million mark. Jiffpom's owner posts snapshots of the fluffy little dog dressed in cute outfits and Jiffpom even has a website. The Pomeranian from the United States has other records to boast of, too. At one time, he held the record for the fastest dog to cover a distance of 16.4 feet on his front legs (7.76 seconds). Another time, he was the record holder for covering 32.8 feet on his hind legs (6.56 seconds).

cat with the most Instagram followers
NALA CAT

In January 2020, and with a total of 4.3 million followers, Nala Cat broke the Guinness World Record for the cat with the most followers on Instagram. By June 2020, the popular feline's record had risen to 4.4 million. Adopted from a shelter at just five months old, the Siamese-Tabby charms online viewers around the world with her bright blue eyes and supercute headgear.

High Tech

TETRIS

best-selling video game ever

Tetris, developed by Russian computer scientist Alexey Pajitnov in 1984, has sold over 500 million copies worldwide—more than any other game. It has been available on almost every video game console since its creation and has seen a resurgence in sales as an app for cell phones and tablets. The iconic puzzle game was the first video game to be exported from the Soviet Union to the United States, the first to be played in outer space, and is often listed as one of the best video games of all time. In 2019, Nintendo released *Tetris 99* for Nintendo Switch—a multiplayer version of the game that sees ninety-nine players compete online.

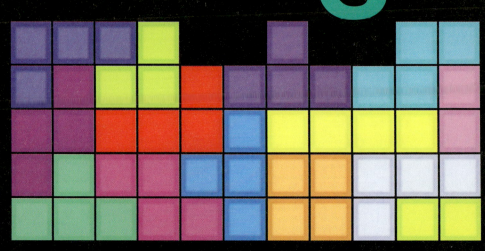

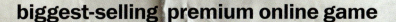

biggest-selling premium online game

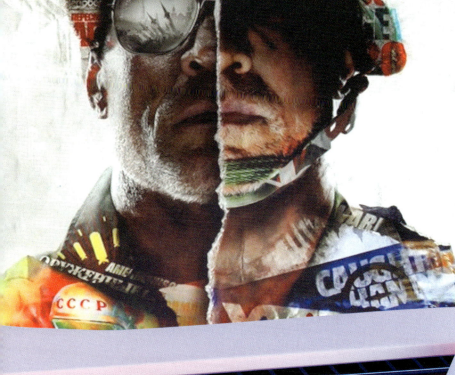

Despite having been released only in November 2020, *Call of Duty: Black Ops Cold War* quickly made history as one of the country's top-selling games, hitting the top 20 all-time list with only a couple months of sales. The game made $678 million in its first six weeks to become 2020's biggest-selling online game, building on more than a decade of success for the franchise. *Call of Duty* has generated $27 billion since its inception in 2003, according to Activision. The entire gaming industry saw a boost from the onset of the COVID-19 pandemic, with people having more time indoors adding up to more money spent on games.

High Tech

best-selling console of all time
PS2

PlayStation's legendary console, the PS2, is still the best-selling console of all time, with parent company Sony confirming the sale of more than 155 million units. Launched in 2000, the PS2 was particularly successful because it could play PS2 games, PS1 games, and even DVDs. More modern consoles have struggled to match the PS2's success; in fact, the majority of the top 10 best-selling consoles are more than a decade old. In second place, with around 154 million units sold, is the Nintendo DS, released in 2004, and in third place is 1989's classic Game Boy, which sold 118.69 million units before it was discontinued fourteen years later.

best-selling video game franchise of all time
MARIO

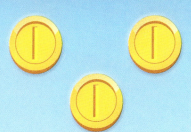

Nintendo's *Mario* franchise has sold 740 million units since the first game was released in 1981. Since then, Mario, his brother Luigi, and other characters like Princess Peach and Yoshi have become household names, starring in a number of games. In the early games, like *Super Mario World*, players jump over obstacles, collect tokens, and capture flags as Mario journeys through the Mushroom Kingdom to save the princess. The franchise has since diversified to include other popular games, such as *Mario Kart*, a racing game showcasing the inhabitants and landscapes of Mushroom Kingdom.

BEST-SELLING VIDEO GAME FRANCHISES
Units sold in millions

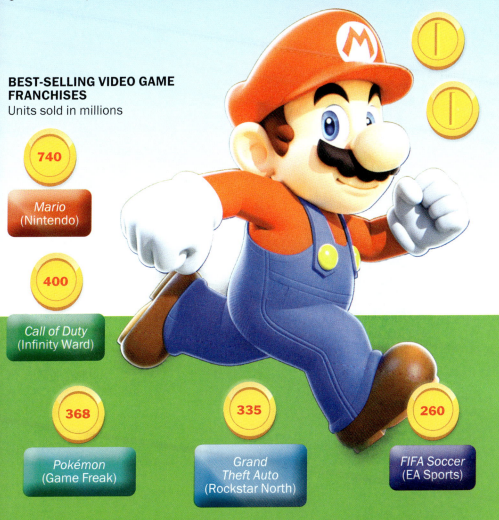

740 — *Mario* (Nintendo)
400 — *Call of Duty* (Infinity Ward)
368 — *Pokémon* (Game Freak)
335 — *Grand Theft Auto* (Rockstar North)
260 — *FIFA Soccer* (EA Sports)

 High Tech

biggest convention for a single video game

MINE

According to Guinness World Records, Minefaire 2016, a gathering of *Minecraft* fans, was the biggest convention ever for a single video game. Held October 15–16, at the Greater Philadelphia Expo Center in Oaks, Pennsylvania, the event attracted 12,140 people. Game developer Markus Persson created *Minecraft* in 2009 and sold it to Microsoft in 2014 for $2.5 billion. Gamers can play alone or with other players online. The game involves breaking and placing blocks to build whatever gamers can imagine—from simple constructions to huge virtual worlds. Attendance was not the only element of Minefaire to gain world-record status. On October 15, the largest-ever *Minecraft* architecture lesson attracted 342 attendees, and American gamer Lestat Wade broke the record for building the tallest staircase in *Minecraft* in one minute.

MINEFAIRE STATS:

12,140 **Number** of people
attending Minefaire: 12,140

150,000 **Total area**, in
square feet, of Minecraft-centered
attractions: 150,000

3 **Number** of Guinness World
Records broken at the fair: 3

CRAFT

2016

High Tech

most popular beauty and style vlogger
YUYA

TOP BEAUTY AND STYLE VLOGGERS
Subscribers in millions (as of January 2021)

24.6	16.7	15	13.8	11.1
Yuya	Jeffree Star	Musas	NikkieTutorials	Zoella

The Mexican vlogger Mariand Castrejón Castañeda, aka Yuya, ranks as YouTube's most popular beauty vlogger based on channel subscriptions. Yuya has more than twenty-four million subscribers. According to Social Blade—YouTube's stats website—she can make up to $108,000 a year from her videos, which get up to 2.5 million views a month. The young woman started her channel in 2009 after winning a makeup video contest. Since that time, she has posted numerous videos on women's beauty and has released her own line of makeup.

world's smallest surgical robot
VERSIUS

British robot specialists Cambridge Medical Robotics developed the world's smallest surgical robot in 2017. Operated by a surgeon using a console guide with a 3-D screen, the robot is able to carry out keyhole surgery. The scientists modeled the robot, called Versius, on the human arm, giving it similar wrist joints to allow maximum flexibility. Keyhole surgery involves making very small cuts on the surface of a person's body, through which a surgeon can operate. The recovery time of the patient is usually quicker when operated on in this way.

biggest walking robot
FANNY

Fanny is a massive 26-foot-high, 51-foot-long, fire-breathing dragon. She is also the world's biggest walking robot. In 2012, a German company designed and built Fanny using both hydraulic and electronic parts. She is radio remote-controlled with nine controllers, while 238 sensors allow the robot to assess her environment. She does this while walking on her four legs or stretching wings that span 39 feet. Powered by a 140-horsepower diesel engine, Fanny weighs a hefty 24,250 pounds—as much as two elephants—and breathes real fire using 24 pounds of liquid gas.

FANNY STATS:

09/27/2012
Date of Fanny's launch

26′ 10″ Fanny's **height**: in feet and inches

51′ 6″ Fanny's **length**: in feet and inches

12′ Fanny's body **width**: in feet

39′ Fanny's **wingspan**: in feet

THE HAPPIEST JABS ON EARTH
Most surprising vaccination site

After around ten months of closure, Disneyland California opened up again in January 2021 . . . as the county's first "super POD" vaccination site, with white tents set up inside with stations for the vaccine to be administered. By the time it closed at the end of April, the site had delivered around 221,000 shots of the vaccine. Other surprising locations for vaccination centers around the world included London's Science Museum and Citi Field, the New York Mets' baseball stadium.

COVID-19 trending

When the COVID-19 lockdown restricted many residents in Llandudno, Wales, to their homes, the town streets filled with some surprising replacements. A herd of 122 wild Kashmiri goats were seen entering the town, eating shrubbery, and exploring people's gardens. The goats often come down to the seaside town from Great Orme, a nearby limestone headland, when the weather is bad, but they seem to have been emboldened by the empty streets to explore farther than before.

SPECIAL VISITORS
Goats take Llandudno

SPEEDY SCIENCE
Fastest vaccine ever developed

Scientists around the world responded quickly to COVID-19, with the fastest development of vaccines in history. Moderna, a US company, began vaccine safety trials only five days after WHO declared the pandemic. A year after the pandemic started, vaccines created by teams in Russia, China, the UK, Europe, the US, and Australia had all been approved for use. By May 2021, several countries had even managed to administer a first dose of a vaccine to more than one-third of their populations.

NOT JUST FOR HUMANS
Endangered ferrets get their shots

Humans aren't the only animals who can get COVID-19—as proven by outbreaks of the disease on mink fur farms. In fall 2020, scientists took the initiative to try to protect ferrets (a relative of the mink) from the virus, injecting 120 endangered black-footed ferrets in Colorado with vaccines. Not all animals seem to be affected by the virus in the same way, however. There are no plans to vaccinate household pets, though zoos have pushed for vaccines to be developed and administered to other endangered species.

ANTI-VIRAL
Will Smith Wipes It Down

According to TikTok, actor Will Smith had the fifth most viral video of 2020 on the app, in part thanks to the need to sanitize surfaces during the COVID-19 pandemic. Smith took part in the "Wipe It Down" challenge, which uses BMW Kenny's rap of the same name and shows participants cleaning a mirror to the beat, with one wipe revealing a different reflection. As of March 2020, it had more than 19 million likes.

109

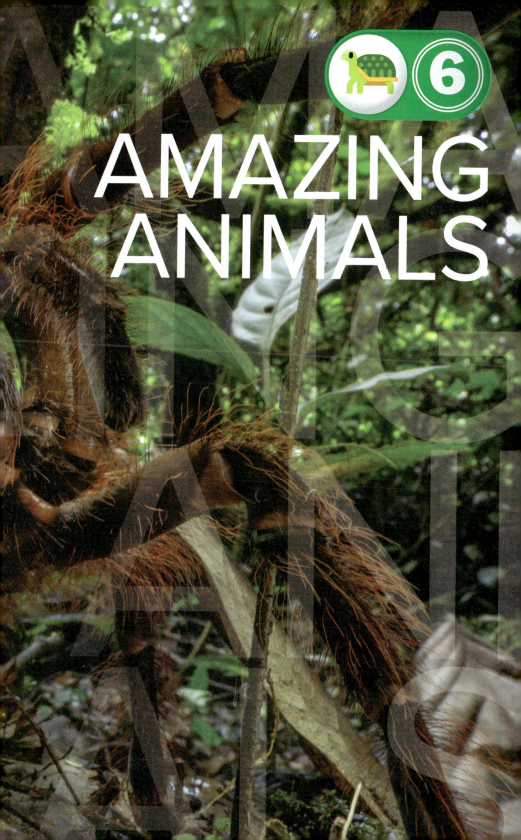

AMAZING ANIMALS

6

BABY BOOM
Ugandan gorilla population soars

The COVID-19 lockdown had a silver lining in Uganda. According to the Uganda Wildlife Authority, with fewer people disturbing natural habitats, mountain gorillas living in the wild saw a rise in population. While an average year would see one or two new births for the country, seven baby gorillas were born between January and September of 2020. This is continuing good news for the subspecies, which was downgraded from "critically endangered" to "endangered" in 2018.

UNLIKELY BFFS
Orangutans and otters make friends

In March 2020, a Belgian zoo made the news after it posted adorable snaps on Facebook of the animals interacting with each other, capturing the hearts of animal lovers around the world. Zookeepers at Pairi Daiza arranged the zoo's habitats so that a family of orangutans (named Ujian, Sari, and Berani) and a romp of Asian small-clawed otters could play together. The otters live in a river that flows through the orangutan habitat and help to provide the clever orangutans with much-needed entertainment and mental stimulation.

 Amazing Animals

trending

LONE SURVIVOR?
Pygmy possum escapes fires

Australia's 2019–2020 bushfire season was catastrophic for wildlife, killing or displacing more than three billion animals. Many feared that this season might be the last for the critically endangered mountain pygmy possum, until conservationists discovered one of the thumb-size animals on Kangaroo Island in December. Only 113 members of the species have ever been recorded, but Australian conservationists are doing their best to preserve their numbers.

LONG-HAUL FLIGHT
Longest nonstop bird migration

A bar-tailed godwit set a record for the longest known nonstop migration in 2020—flying from Alaska to New Zealand over eleven days without stopping. The bird was tracked on its 7,500-mile journey by a satellite tag, after being caught and tagged in 2019. Godwits are known for their endurance flying, even shrinking their internal organs to make themselves lighter for the long journey!

G(IRAFFE)-P-S
Rare giraffe gets tracking device

As far as we know, there is only one white giraffe currently living on Earth—making it extremely rare! The white giraffe, which lives on the Ishaqbini Hirola Community Conservancy in eastern Kenya, has a genetic condition called leucism, which reduces the amount of melanin pigment it has. In 2020, conservationists fitted this special specimen with a GPS tracking device to help deter poachers.

Amazing Animals

world's sleepiest animal
KOALA

Australia's koala sleeps for up to twenty hours a day and still manages to look sleepy when awake. This is due to the koala's unbelievably monotonous diet. It feeds, mostly at night, on the aromatic leaves of eucalyptus trees. The leaves have little nutritional or calorific value, so the marsupial saves energy by snoozing. It jams its rear end into a fork in the branches of its favorite tree so it cannot fall out while snoozing.

world's best glider
FLYING SQUIRREL

Flying squirrels are champion animal gliders. The Japanese giant flying squirrel has been scientifically recorded making flights over distances of up to 164 feet from tree to tree. These creatures have been estimated to make 656-foot flights when flying downhill.

The squirrel remains aloft using a special flap of skin on either side of its body, which stretches between wrist and ankle. Its fluffy tail acts as a stabilizer to keep it steady, and the squirrel changes direction by twisting its wrists and moving its limbs.

WORLD'S GLIDERS
Distance in feet

- Flying squirrel
- Flying fish
- Colugo, or flying lemur
- Draco, or flying lizard
- Flying squid

164 197 230 655 656

 Amazing Animals

The African bush elephant is the world's largest living land animal. The biggest known bush elephant stood 13.8 feet at the shoulder and had an estimated weight of 13.5 tons. It is also the animal with the largest outer ears. The outsize flappers help keep the animal cool on the open savanna. The Asian elephant has much smaller earflaps, because it lives in the forest and is not exposed to the same high temperatures.

world's heaviest land mammal
AFRICAN BUSH ELEPHANT

world's tiniest bat
KITTI'S HOG-NOSED BAT

This little critter, the Kitti's hog-nosed bat, is just 1.3 inches long, with a wingspan of 6.7 inches, and weighs 0.07–0.10 ounces. It's tied for first place as the world's smallest mammal with Savi's pygmy shrew, which is longer at 2.1 inches but lighter at 0.04–0.06 ounces. The bat lives in west central Thailand and southeast Myanmar, and the shrew is found from the Mediterranean to Southeast Asia.

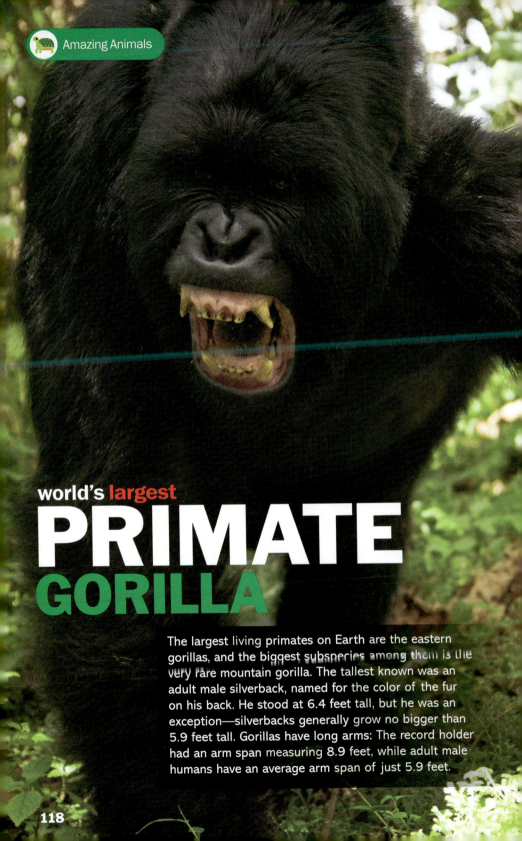

Amazing Animals

world's largest
PRIMATE
GORILLA

The largest living primates on Earth are the eastern gorillas, and the biggest subspecies among them is the very rare mountain gorilla. The tallest known was an adult male silverback, named for the color of the fur on his back. He stood at 6.4 feet tall, but he was an exception—silverbacks generally grow no bigger than 5.9 feet tall. Gorillas have long arms: The record holder had an arm span measuring 8.9 feet, while adult male humans have an average arm span of just 5.9 feet.

world's most
COLORFUL
monkey
MANDRILL

The male mandrill's face is as flamboyant as his rear end. The vivid colors of both are brightest at breeding time. The colors announce to his rivals that he is an alpha male and he has the right to breed with the females. His exceptionally long and fang-like canine teeth reinforce his dominance. The mandrill is the world's largest monkey, as well as the most colorful.

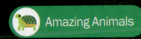 Amazing Animals

FASTEST LAND ANIMALS
Top speed

Cheetah: **61 mph**

Ostrich: **60 mph**

Pronghorn: **55 mph**

Springbok: **55 mph**

Lion: **30 mph**

world's fastest land animal
CHEETAH

The fastest reliably recorded running speed of any animal was that of a zoo-bred cheetah that reached an incredible 61 miles per hour on a flat surface. The record was achieved in 2012, from a standing start by a captive cheetah at Cincinnati Zoo.

More recently, wild cheetahs have been timed while actually hunting their prey in the bush in Botswana. Using GPS technology and special tracking collars, the scientists found that these cheetahs had a top speed of 58 miles per hour over rough terrain.

120

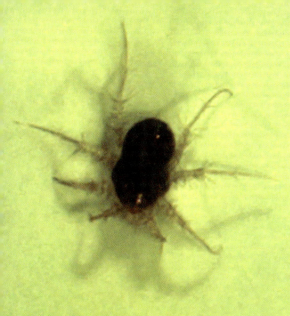

world's
FASTEST animal
PARATARSOTOMUS MACROPALPIS

Step aside, cheetah! A tiny mite, just 0.028 inches long but with the ginormous name *Paratarsotomus macropalpis*, has set a new record for the fastest-running terrestrial animal ever, according to Stanford University. The mite can run twenty times faster than a cheetah, size for size, and can even outrun the previous record holder—the Australian tiger beetle. While the beetle can whiz along at 171 body lengths per second and the cheetah 16 body lengths per second, the mite achieves an astonishing 322 body lengths per second at top speed. That's the equivalent of Olympic champion Usain Bolt racing at 1,400 miles per hour!

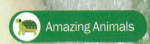 Amazing Animals

world's largest BIG CAT TIGER

There are only five big cats that roam the Earth: tiger, lion, jaguar, leopard, and snow leopard. The biggest and heaviest is the Siberian, or Amur, tiger, which lives in the taiga (boreal forest) of eastern Siberia, where it hunts deer and wild boar. The largest reliably measured tigers have been about 11.8 feet long and weighed 705 pounds, but there have been claims for larger individuals, such as the male shot in the Sikhote-Alin Mountains in 1950. That tiger weighed 847 pounds.

world's noisiest land animal
HOWLER MONKEY

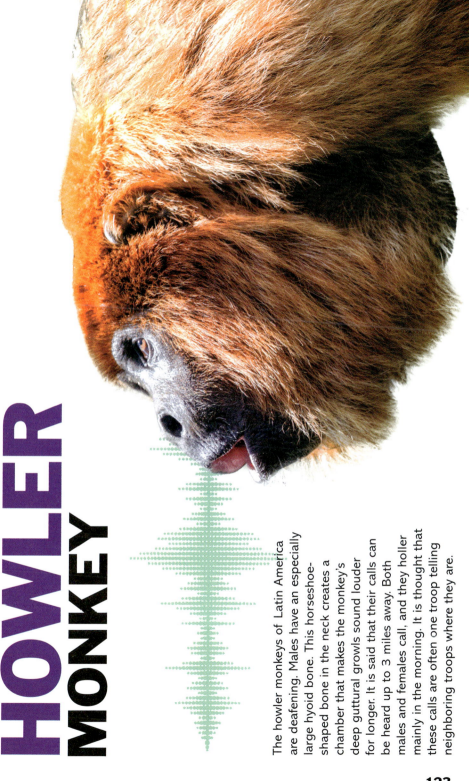

The howler monkeys of Latin America are deafening. Males have an especially large hyoid bone. This horseshoe-shaped bone in the neck creates a chamber that makes the monkey's deep guttural growls sound louder for longer. It is said that their calls can be heard up to 3 miles away. Both males and females call, and they holler mainly in the morning. It is thought that these calls are often one troop telling neighboring troops where they are.

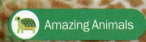 Amazing Animals

GIRAFFE STATS

6 HEIGHT OF A CALF AT BIRTH (in feet)

25 AVERAGE LIFE SPAN (in years)

100 ADULT'S DAILY FOOD CONSUMPTION (in pounds of leaves and twigs)

Giraffes living on the savannas of eastern and southern Africa are the world's tallest animals. The tallest known bull giraffe measured 19 feet from the ground to the top of his horns. He could have looked over the top of a London double-decker bus or peered into the upstairs window of a two-story house. Despite having considerably longer necks than we do, giraffes have the same number of neck vertebrae. They also have long legs with which they can either speedily escape from predators or kick them to keep them away.

REACHING GREAT HEIGHTS

A giraffe's tongue can grow up to 21 inches in length. This helps the animal reach leaves on the topmost branches of a tree when it is looking for food.

GIRAFFE
world's tallest living animal

 Amazing Animals

world's longest tooth
NARWHAL

The narwhal's "sword" is an enormously elongated spiral tooth, or tusk. In male narwhals it can grow to more than 8.2 feet long. Only about 15 percent of females grow a tusk, which typically is smaller than a male tusk, with a less noticeable spiral. It has been suggested that the tusk serves as an adornment to attract the opposite sex—the larger a male narwhal's tusk, the more attractive he is to females. It is also thought to be a sensory organ that detects changes in the seawater, such as saltiness, which could help the narwhal find food. Observers have also noted that the narwhal uses its tusk to stun prey.

the world's largest living animal
BLUE WHALE

Blue whales are truly colossal. The largest one accurately measured was 110 feet long, and the heaviest weighed 209 tons. They feed on tiny krill, which they filter from the sea. On land, the largest known animal was a Titanosaur—a huge dinosaur that lived 101 million years ago in what is now Argentina. A skeleton found in 2014 suggests the creature was 121 feet long and weighed 77 tons. It belongs to a young Titanosaur, so an adult may have been bigger than a blue whale.

Amazing Animals

world's biggest
FISH
WHALE SHARK

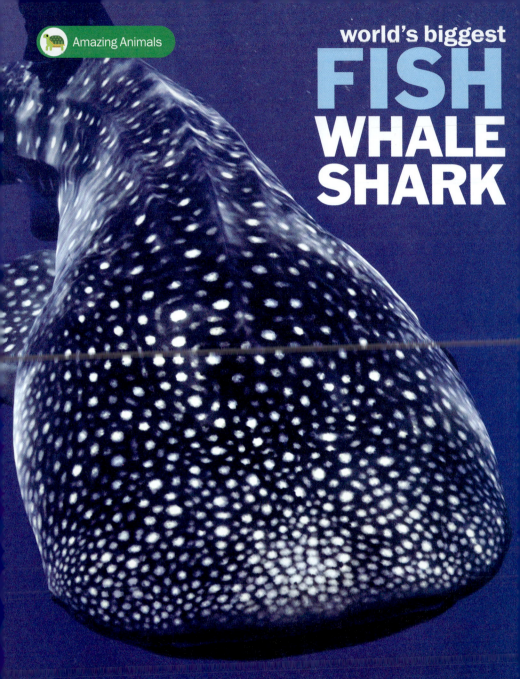

Recognizable from its spotted skin and enormous size, the whale shark is the world's largest living fish. It grows to a maximum length of about 66 feet. Like the blue whale, this fish feeds on some of the smallest creatures: krill, marine larvae, small fish, and fish eggs.

The whale shark is also a great traveler: One female was tracked swimming 4,800 miles from Mexico—where hundreds of whale sharks gather each summer to feed—to the middle of the South Atlantic Ocean, where it is thought she may have given birth.

the shark most dangerous to people
GREAT WHITE SHARK

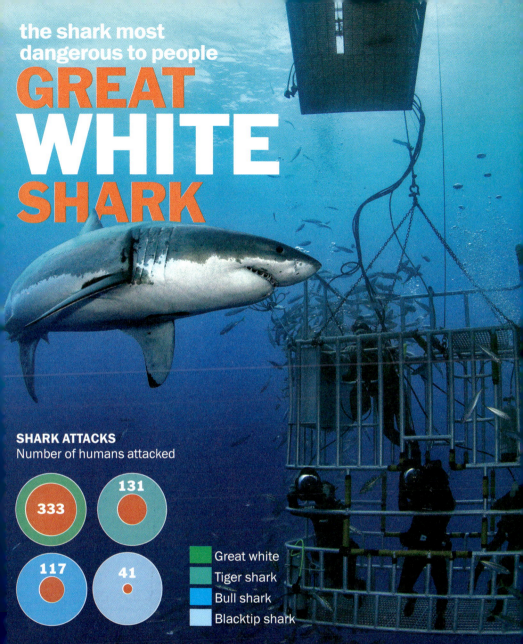

SHARK ATTACKS
Number of humans attacked

- 333 Great white
- 131 Tiger shark
- 117 Bull shark
- 41 Blacktip shark

The great white shark is at the top of the list for the highest number of attacks on people. The largest reliably measured fish was 21 feet long, making it the largest predatory fish in the sea. Its jaws are lined with large, triangular, serrated teeth that can slice through flesh, sinew, and even bone. However, there were just fifty-seven reported unprovoked attacks by sharks of any kind in 2020, and ten of those proved fatal. Humans are not this creature's top food of choice. People don't have enough fat on their bodies. Mature white sharks prefer blubber-rich seals, dolphins, and whales. It is likely that many of the attacks on people are probably cases of mistaken identity.

Amazing Animals

KOMODO DRAGON

world's largest lizard

There are dragons on Indonesia's Komodo Island, and they're dangerous. The Komodo dragon's jaws are lined with sixty replaceable, serrated, backward-pointing teeth. Its saliva is laced with deadly bacteria and venom that the dragon works into a wound, ensuring its prey will die quickly. Prey can be as big as a pig or deer, because this lizard is the world's largest. It can grow up to 10.3 feet long and weigh 366 pounds.

world's deadliest frog
POISON DART FROG

A poison dart frog's skin exudes toxins. There are several species, and the more vivid a frog's color, the more deadly its poison. The skin color warns potential predators that the frogs are not good to eat, although one snake is immune to the chemicals and happily feeds on these creatures. It is thought that the frogs do not manufacture their own poisons, but obtain the chemicals from their diet of ants, millipedes, and mites. The most deadly species to people is also the largest, Colombia's golden poison dart frog. At just one inch long, a single frog has enough poison to kill ten to twenty people.

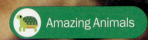 Amazing Animals

The saltwater crocodile, or "saltie," is the world's largest living reptile. Males can grow to over 20 feet long, but a few old-timers become real monsters. A well-known crocodile in the Segama River, Borneo, left an impression on a sandbank that measured 33 feet. The saltie can be found in areas from eastern India to northeast Australia, where it lives in mangroves, estuaries, and rivers. It is sometimes found out at sea. The saltie is an ambush predator, grabbing any animal that enters its domain—including people. Saltwater crocodiles account for twenty to thirty attacks on people per year, up to half of which are fatal.

world's largest reptile
SALTWATER CROCODILE

"Saltie" crocodiles can live for up to 70 years in the wild.

world's smallest owl
NORTH AMERICAN ELF OWL

The North American elf owl is one of three tiny owls vying for this title. It is about 5 inches long and weighs 1.5 ounces. This owl spends winter in Mexico and flies to nest in Arizona and New Mexico in spring. It often occupies cavities excavated by woodpeckers in saguaro cacti. Rivals for the title of smallest owl are Peru's long-whiskered owlet and Mexico's Tamaulipas pygmy owl, which are both a touch shorter but slightly heavier, making the elf owl the smallest of all.

FIVE OF THE WORLD'S OWLS
Height in inches

- North American elf owl
- Little owl
- Barn owl
- Snowy owl
- Great gray owl

33

28

15

8.7

5

Amazing Animals

world's smelliest bird
HOATZIN

The hoatzin eats leaves, flowers, and fruit. It ferments the food in its crop (a pouch in its esophagus). This habit leaves the bird with a foul odor, which has led people to nickname the hoatzin the "stinkbird." About the size of a pheasant, this bird lives in the Amazon and Orinoco river basins of South America. A hoatzin chick has sharp claws on its wings, like a pterodactyl. If threatened by a snake, the chick jumps from the nest into the water, then uses its wing claws to help it climb back up.

bird with the longest tail
RIBBON-TAILED ASTRAPIA

The ribbon-tailed astrapia has the longest feathers in relation to body size of any wild bird. The male, which has a beautiful, iridescent blue-green head, sports a pair of white ribbon-shaped tail feathers that are more than 3.3 feet long—three times the length of its 13-inch-long body. It is one of Papua New Guinea's birds of paradise and lives in the mountain forests of central New Guinea, where males sometimes have to untangle their tails from the foliage before they can fly.

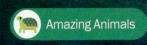 Amazing Animals

bird that builds largest nest
BALD EAGLE

THE WORLD'S LARGEST NESTS
Diameter in inches
- Bald eagle
- White stork
- Golden eagle

114
57
55

With a wingspan over 6.6 feet, bald eagles need space to land and take off—so their nests can be gargantuan. Over the years, a nest built by a pair of bald eagles in St. Petersburg, Florida, has taken on epic proportions. Measuring 9.5 feet across and 20 feet deep, it is made of sticks, grass, and moss. At one stage it was thought to have weighed at least 2 tons, making it the largest nest ever constructed by a pair of birds. Although one pair nests at a time, these huge structures are often the work of several pairs of birds, each building on top of the work of their predecessors.

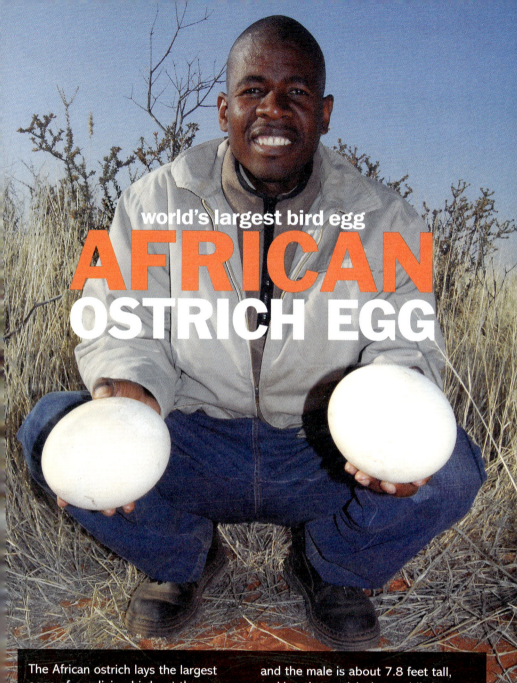

world's largest bird egg
AFRICAN OSTRICH EGG

The African ostrich lays the largest eggs of any living bird, yet they are the smallest eggs relative to the size of the mother's body. Each egg is some 5.9 inches long and weighs about 3.5–5 pounds, while the mother is about 6.2 feet tall and the male is about 7.8 feet tall, making the ostrich the world's largest living bird. The female lays about fifty eggs per year, and each egg contains as much yolk and albumen as twenty-four hens' eggs. It takes an hour to soft boil an ostrich egg!

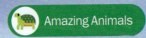 Amazing Animals

EMPEROR PENGUIN STATS

80 **AVERAGE WEIGHT OF AN ADULT**: 80 pounds

1,640 **DEPTH AN ADULT CAN SWIM TO**: 1,640 feet

22 **LENGTH OF TIME UNDERWATER**: Up to 22 minutes

world's biggest penguin
EMPEROR PENGUIN

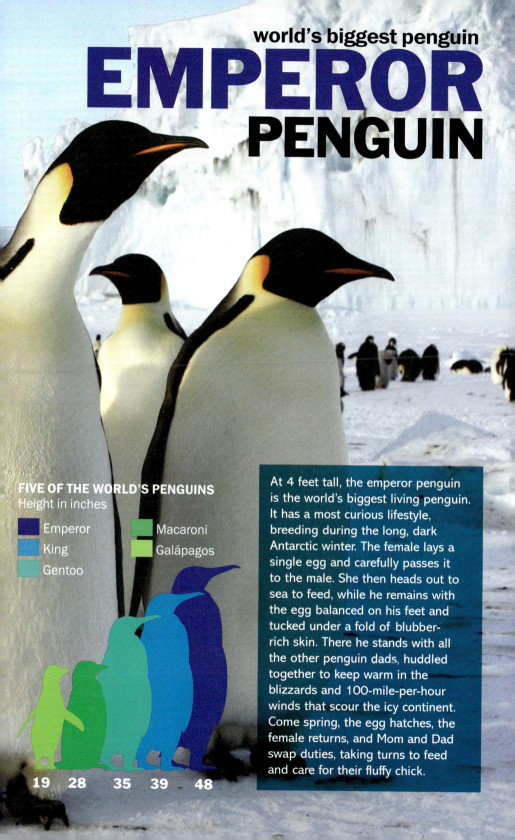

FIVE OF THE WORLD'S PENGUINS
Height in inches

- Emperor
- King
- Gentoo
- Macaroni
- Galápagos

19 28 35 39 48

At 4 feet tall, the emperor penguin is the world's biggest living penguin. It has a most curious lifestyle, breeding during the long, dark Antarctic winter. The female lays a single egg and carefully passes it to the male. She then heads out to sea to feed, while he remains with the egg balanced on his feet and tucked under a fold of blubber-rich skin. There he stands with all the other penguin dads, huddled together to keep warm in the blizzards and 100-mile-per-hour winds that scour the icy continent. Come spring, the egg hatches, the female returns, and Mom and Dad swap duties, taking turns to feed and care for their fluffy chick.

Amazing Animals

FOUR OF THE WORLD'S SPIDERS
Leg span in inches

- Giant huntsman spider
- Goliath bird-eating tarantula
- Brazilian wandering spider
- Golden silk orb-weaver

12 · 11 · 5.9 · 5 · 5 · 5.9 · 11 · 12

GOLIATH BIRD-EATING TARANTULA
world's heaviest spider

The size of a dinner plate, the female goliath bird-eating tarantula has a leg span of 11 inches and weighs up to 6.17 ounces. This is the world's heaviest spider and a real nightmare for an arachnophobe (someone with a fear of spiders). Its fangs can pierce a person's skin, but its venom is no worse than a bee sting. The hairs on its body are more of a hazard. When threatened, it rubs its abdomen with its hind legs and releases tiny hairs that cause severe irritation to the skin. Despite its name, this spider does not actually eat birds very often.

140

world's biggest penguin
EMPEROR PENGUIN

FIVE OF THE WORLD'S PENGUINS
Height in inches

- Emperor
- King
- Gentoo
- Macaroni
- Galápagos

19 28 35 39 48

At 4 feet tall, the emperor penguin is the world's biggest living penguin. It has a most curious lifestyle, breeding during the long, dark Antarctic winter. The female lays a single egg and carefully passes it to the male. She then heads out to sea to feed, while he remains with the egg balanced on his feet and tucked under a fold of blubber-rich skin. There he stands with all the other penguin dads, huddled together to keep warm in the blizzards and 100-mile-per-hour winds that scour the icy continent. Come spring, the egg hatches, the female returns, and Mom and Dad swap duties, taking turns to feed and care for their fluffy chick.

Amazing Animals

GOLIATH BIRD-EATING TARANTULA

world's heaviest spider

The size of a dinner plate, the female goliath bird-eating tarantula has a leg span of 11 inches and weighs up to 6.17 ounces. This is the world's heaviest spider and a real nightmare for an arachnophobe (someone with a fear of spiders). Its fangs can pierce a person's skin, but its venom is no worse than a bee sting. The hairs on its body are more of a hazard. When threatened, it rubs its abdomen with its hind legs and releases tiny hairs that cause severe irritation to the skin. Despite its name, this spider does not actually eat birds very often.

FOUR OF THE WORLD'S SPIDERS
Leg span in inches

- Giant huntsman spider
- Goliath bird-eating tarantula
- Brazilian wandering spider
- Golden silk orb-weaver

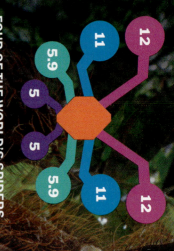

12 · 11 · 5.9 · 5 · 5 · 5.9 · 11 · 12

Flying insects are difficult to clock, and many impressive speeds have been claimed. The fastest airspeed reliably timed was by fifteen desert locusts that managed an average of 21 miles per hour. Airspeed is the actual speed at which the insect flies. It is different from ground speed, which is often enhanced by favorable winds. A black cutworm moth whizzed along at 70 miles per hour while riding the winds ahead of a cold front. The most shocking measurement, however, is that of a horsefly with an estimated airspeed of 90 miles per hour while chasing an air-gun pellet! The speed, understandably, has not been verified.

world's fastest flying insect

DESERT LOCUST

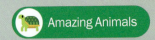
Amazing Animals

world's deadliest animal
MOSQUITO

Female mosquitoes live on the blood of birds and mammals—humans included. However, the problem is not what they take, but what they leave behind. In some mosquitoes' saliva are organisms that cause the world's most deadly illnesses, including malaria, yellow fever, dengue fever, West Nile virus, and encephalitis. It is estimated that mosquitoes transmit diseases to 700 million people every year, of which 725,000 die. Mosquitoes are the deadliest family of insects on earth.

world's longest insect migration
GLOBE
SKIMMER

Each year millions of dragonflies fly thousands of miles across the Indian Ocean from Southern India to East Africa. Most of them are globe skimmers, a species known to fly long distances and at altitudes up to 3,280 feet. They can travel 2,175 miles in 24 hours. Coral cays on the way have little open fresh water so the insects stay there for a few days before moving on to East Africa. Here, they follow the rains, at each stop taking advantage of temporary rainwater pools to lay their eggs to hatch where their young can rapidly develop. Four generations are involved in a round trip of about 11,000 miles— farther than the distance from New York to Sydney.

FISHY BUSINESS
Most expensive tropical fish

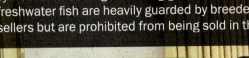

The Asian arowana is currently the world's most expensive aquarium fish. Because red is associated with wealth, the redder the fish, the higher the price—one can cost up to $300,000! The arowana has become a status symbol and is thought to bring good luck. These pricey freshwater fish are heavily guarded by breeders and sellers but are prohibited from being sold in the US.

RODENT SUPERHERO
Rat sniffs out landmines

In 2020, Magawa became the first rat to receive a gold medal from the People's Dispensary for Sick Animals. The award, given to civilian animals for "outstanding acts of devotion or valor," was in recognition of Magawa's work in Cambodia, where he helped to clear more than 169,000 square yards of land, having been trained to sniff out explosive chemicals. Rats are used for this because they are too light to trigger the landmines and can work quickly and efficiently.

THE OVAL PAWFFICE
First Pets enjoy their new home

The inauguration of the forty-sixth US president brought two German shepherds named Champ and Major to the White House. They made headlines in January 2021, when a fan account created a press release supposedly from the First Dogs, expressing their plans for their new home. The account behind #DOTUS has amassed over 215,000 followers on Twitter, keeping fans updated on sightings of the First Pets in and around the White House. Sadly, Champ passed away in June 2021, aged thirteen.

trending

LLAMA DRAMA
Gizmo goes wild

Gizmo the llama made news in 2020 when he escaped his new farm in Westchester County, New York. A day after their arrival in Bedford Corners, Gizmo and his llama companion, Sandman, jumped the fence. His friend was brought home safely, but Gizmo evaded his new owners, sparking a search by both land and air to bring him home. He was found safe and well after sixteen days by some maintenance workers who recognized him from posters put up around the town.

Amazing Pets

@MINNESOTADUCK
Duck with the most Instagram followers

The duck with the most followers on Instagram is Ben Afquack, who lives in St. Paul, Minnesota. His owner, Derek Johnson, runs the popular account, featuring videos of Ben walking around town and "helping" his owners work out. The Instagram had 79,002 followers when Ben's title was certified by Guinness World Records. Viral videos of Ben drumming with his feet have solidified his celebrity status, and the feathered sensation now even has his own line of merchandise.

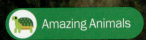 Amazing Animals

ANGORA RABBIT
world's fluffiest rabbit

In most people's opinion, the Angora rabbit is the world's fluffiest bunny. The breed originated in Turkey and is thought to be one of the world's oldest rabbit breeds as well. It became popular with the French court in the mid-eighteenth century. Today it is bred for its long, soft, wool, which is shorn every three to four months. One of the fluffiest bunnies is buff-colored Franchesca, owned by English Angora rabbit expert Dr. Betty Chu. In 2014, Franchesca's fur was measured at 14.3 inches, making a world record that is yet to be beaten.

world's smallest horse
BOMBEL

Bombel is a miniature Appaloosa living in Poland. At just 22 inches from the bottom of his hooves to the top of his shoulder blades, he is the world's shortest living stallion. According to the American Miniature Horse Association, a "mini-horse" must be less than 38 inches tall at the withers, so Bombel more than qualifies. Bombel gets his name, meaning "Bubble," on account of his plump body and exceedingly short legs. Once a month, he visits children in the local hospital. However, Bombel is not the shortest horse of all time. That was Thumbelina, a sorrel brown mare from St. Louis, Missouri. She measured 17.5 inches at the shoulder.

> Amazing Animals

world's hairiest dog
KOMONDOR

The world's hairiest dog breed is the Komondor, or Hungarian sheepdog. It is a powerful dog that was bred originally to guard sheep. Its long, white, dreadlock-like "cords" enable it not only to blend in with the flock but also to protect itself from bad weather and bites from wolves. This is a large dog, standing over 27.5 inches at the shoulders. Its hairs are up to 10.6 inches long, giving it the heaviest coat of any dog.

America's most popular dog breed
LABRADOR

The Labrador Retriever holds the top spot as America's most popular dog breed for a 30th consecutive year. Its eager-to-please temperament makes it an ideal companion. The Labrador was originally bred as a gun dog that fetched game birds shot by hunters. Now, aside from being a family pet, it is both a favored assistance dog that helps blind people and a good detection dog used by law-enforcement agencies. A newcomer to the list, the Dachshund ousts the Pembroke Welsh Corgi to claim spot no. 10.

AMERICA'S MOST POPULAR DOGS

Rating
1. Labrador Retriever
2. French Bulldog
3. German Shepherd
4. Golden Retriever
5. Bulldog
6. Poodle
7. Beagle
8. Rottweiler
9. German Short-haired Pointer
10. Dachshund

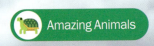

Amazing Animals

world's longest-lived land animal
JONATHAN

Having celebrated his 189th birthday in 2021, Jonathan the tortoise is the world's longest-lived known land animal. He hatched in 1832 or thereabouts on the Aldabra Atoll, part of the Seychelles archipelago in the Indian Ocean. Since 1882, he's been living on a distant island in another ocean—St. Helena, part of a British overseas territory in the South Atlantic—when he was presented to the governor at the time as a gift. Today, he still lives on the lawn in front of Plantation House, the official residence of the Governor of St. Helena, with three other giant tortoises. Jonathan puts his longevity down to a healthy diet of fresh grass and fruit.

world's smallest dog

CHIHUAHUA

Chihuahuas are the world's smallest dog breed—and the smallest of them all is Miracle Milly, a Chihuahua from Puerto Rico. She measures just 3.8 inches tall, no bigger than a sneaker. The shortest is Heaven Sent Brandy from Largo, Florida, just 6 inches from her nose to the tip of her tail. Chihuahuas originated in Mexico and may have predated the Maya. They are probably descendants of the Techichi, an early companion dog of the Toltec civilization (900–1168 CE).

Amazing Animals

WORLD'S MOST POPULAR CATS

Rating
1. Ragdoll
2. Exotic Shorthair
3. Maine Coon Cat
4. Persian
5. British Shorthair
6. Devon Rex
7. Abyssinian
8. American Shorthair
9. Scottish Fold
10. Sphynx

world's most popular cat breed
RAGDOLL

According to the Cat Fanciers' Association, the Ragdoll melted the hearts of American cat lovers in 2020. This is the third year running that the "Raggie" has taken the top spot as the most-registered cat breed of the year. With its lush, silky fur and big blue eyes, this is a cat that loves to be around human beings, relaxing like a "rag doll" when curled up on your lap. The Exotic Shorthair, with its teddy-bear looks, had to settle for second place in the listings.

world's baldest cat
SPHYNX

The sphynx breed of cats is famous for its wrinkles and the lack of a normal coat, but it is not entirely hairless. Its skin is like the **softest chamois** leather, but it has a thin layer of down. It behaves more like a dog than a cat, greeting owners when they come home, and is friendly to strangers. The breed originated in Canada, where a black-and-white cat gave birth to a hairless kitten called Prune in 1966. Subsequent breeding gave rise to the sphynx.

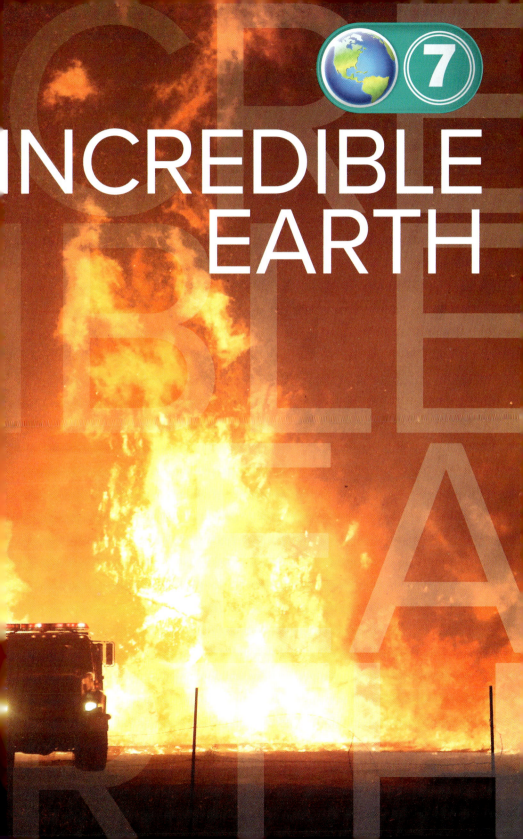
INCREDIBLE EARTH

7

GAMERS GO GREEN
Earth Day's anniversary is celebrated online

Earth Day 2020 was the fiftieth anniversary of the annual event, but the global pandemic meant that organizers had to rethink their plans to celebrate. Instead of an in-person gathering in Washington, DC, organizers took Earth Day online, with a twelve-hour live stream of speakers and music, and partnerships with the gaming community.

Incredible Earth

trending

PRETTY UGLY
New orchid species turns heads

Not all flowers are beautiful—in 2020, the Royal Botanical Gardens in Kew, England, introduced an unsightly new species to the world. *Gastrodia agnicellus*, found in Madagascar, was dubbed the world's ugliest orchid for its brown and fleshy appearance. Kew botanist Johan Hermans, who discovered the orchid, joked, "I'm sure its mother thinks it's very lovely." Due to agriculture and fires in Madagascar, the strange-looking plant has been classified as a threatened species.

@NATGEO
Most popular brand on Instagram

According to Brandwatch, National Geographic is the brand with the most followers on Instagram—not including Instagram itself. The account, @natgeo, shares beautiful and diverse photographs taken by expert photographers, so it's no surprise that the account has over 160 million followers, making it the eleventh most followed account overall on the photo-sharing platform. In 2019, NatGeo became the first brand to hit the milestone of 100 million Instagram followers.

FIRST IN 100 YEARS
Detached coral reef discovered

Scientists at Australia's Schmidt Ocean Institute made an exciting discovery in 2020, when their underwater research vessel *Falkor* came across a detached coral reef. At more than 1,640 feet, it is taller than the Empire State Building, and supports a diverse range of ocean life. The institute released a three-hour live stream on YouTube showing their underwater robot "SuBastian" exploring the reef, with expert commentary.

A GIANT FIND
Titanosaur unearthed in Argentina

An important dinosaur specimen has been uncovered in Neuquén, Argentina. Remains of *Ninjatitan zapatai*, or "Ninja Giant," were first found in 2014, and paleontologists believe that it might be the oldest known species of titanosaur—a group that includes some of the largest creatures to have walked the Earth. Ninja Giant is 65 feet long, and scientists believe that it lived 140 million years ago. If this is true, it would mean that titanosaurs first appeared much longer ago than previously thought.

Incredible Earth

oldest tree on earth
BRISTLECONE PINE

An unnamed bristlecone pine in the White Mountains of California is the world's oldest continually standing tree. It is 5,068 years old, beating its bristlecone rivals the Methuselah (4,862 years old) and Prometheus (4,850 years old). Sweden is home to an even older tree, a Norway spruce (which are often used as Christmas trees) that took root about 9,552 years ago. However, this tree has not been standing continually. It is long lived because it can clone itself. When the trunk dies, a new one grows up from the same rootstock, so in theory it could live forever.

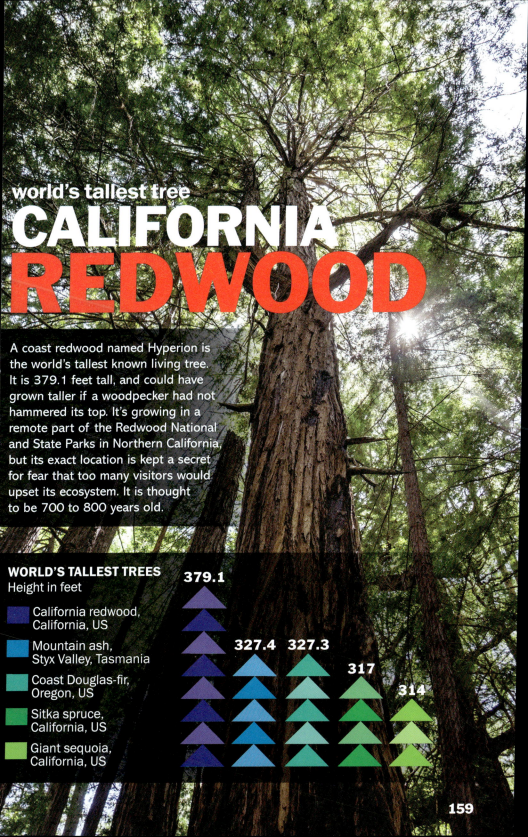

world's tallest tree
CALIFORNIA REDWOOD

A coast redwood named Hyperion is the world's tallest known living tree. It is 379.1 feet tall, and could have grown taller if a woodpecker had not hammered its top. It's growing in a remote part of the Redwood National and State Parks in Northern California, but its exact location is kept a secret for fear that too many visitors would upset its ecosystem. It is thought to be 700 to 800 years old.

WORLD'S TALLEST TREES
Height in feet

- California redwood, California, US — 379.1
- Mountain ash, Styx Valley, Tasmania — 327.4
- Coast Douglas-fir, Oregon, US — 327.3
- Sitka spruce, California, US — 317
- Giant sequoia, California, US — 314

Incredible Earth

largest and heaviest fruit
PUMPKIN

The world's largest and heaviest fruit was a cultivated pumpkin weighing 2,625 pounds. It was grown by Belgian gardener Mathias Willemijns and certified in 2016 at the Giant Pumpkin European Championship in Germany. It's only the second time since 1900 that the title holder was not from North America. The seeds of most giant pumpkins trace their ancestry back to the Mammoth varieties of squash cultivated by Canadian pumpkin breeder Howard Dill in the 1980s.

world's toughest leaf
AMAZON
WATER LILY

The leaf of the giant Amazon water lily can grow as wide as 8.6 feet across. It has an upturned rim and a waxy, water-repellent upper surface. On the underside of the leaf is a riblike structure that traps air, enabling the leaf to float easily. The ribs are also lined with sharp spines that protect them from aquatic plant eaters. A full-grown leaf is so large and so strong that it can support up to 99 pounds in weight.

 Incredible Earth

world's deepest cave
VERYOVKINA

The limestone-rich Western Caucasus region in the Eurasian country of Georgia has some extraordinary cave systems. Among the caverns there is Veryovkina, the deepest cave in the world. It's over 7,257 feet deep! (That's more than sixteen times taller than the Great Pyramid of Giza.) It took as many as thirty expeditions over more than fifty years before Russian cavers reached the record depth, and they suspect there is even more to explore.

EXTRAORDINARY LENGTHS
In order to establish the record-breaking depths of Veryovkina Cave, cavers took three days to get down and three days to return to the surface, resting in subterranean camps along the way.

VERYOVKINA CAVE STATS

1968 YEAR OF DISCOVERY
7,257 DEPTH DISCOVERED TO DATE (in feet)
2018 YEAR CURRENT DEPTH ESTABLISHED

Incredible Earth

DENMAN GLACIER

the deepest point on land

The deepest point on land has been discovered under the Denman Glacier in East Antarctica. Deep below the Antarctic ice sheet, which is 1.3 miles thick on average, there is an ice-filled canyon whose floor is 11,500 feet below sea level. By comparison, the lowest clearly visible point on land is in the Jordan Rift Valley, on the shore of the Dead Sea, just 1,412 feet below sea level. It makes the Denman canyon the deepest canyon on land. Only trenches at the bottom of the ocean are deeper. The floor of the deepest—the Mariana Trench—is close to 7 miles below the sea's surface.

164

world's greatest number of GEYSERS — YELLOWSTONE NATIONAL PARK

There are about 1,000 geysers that erupt worldwide, and 540 of them are in Yellowstone National Park, US. That's the greatest concentration of geysers on Earth. The most famous is Old Faithful, which spews out a cloud of steam and hot water to a maximum height of 185 feet every 44 to 125 minutes. Yellowstone's spectacular water display is due to its closeness to molten rock from Earth's mantle that rises up to the surface. One day the park could face an eruption 1,000 times as powerful as that of Mount St. Helens in 1980.

- 540
- 139
- 84
- 33
- 16

GEYSER FIELDS
Number of geysers

- Yellowstone, Idaho/Montana/Wyoming, US
- Valley of Geysers, Kamchatka, Russia
- El Tatio, Andes, Chile
- Orakei Korako, New Zealand
- Hveravellir, Iceland

165

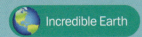

Incredible Earth

earth's tallest mountain above sea level
MOUNT EVEREST

Mount Everest has grown. In December 2020, Nepal and China agreed an official height that is 2.8 feet higher than the previous calculation. The mega mountain is located in the Himalayas, on the border between Tibet and Nepal. The mountain acquired its official name from surveyor Sir George Everest, but local people know it as Chomolungma (Tibet) or Sagarmatha (Nepal). In 1953, Sir Edmund Hillary and Tenzing Norgay were the first people to reach its summit. Now, more than 650 people per year manage to make the spectacular climb.

WORLD'S TALLEST MOUNTAINS
Height above sea level in feet

- Everest
- K2 (Qogir)
- Kanchenjunga
- Lhotse
- Makalu

Everest: 29,032
K2 (Qogir): 28,251
Kanchenjunga: 28,179
Lhotse: 27,940
Makalu: 27,838

world's longest coral reef system
GREAT BARRIER REEF

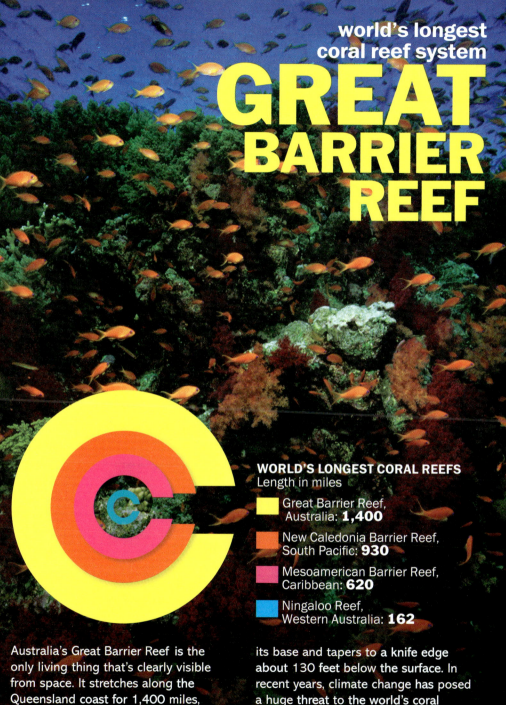

WORLD'S LONGEST CORAL REEFS
Length in miles

- Great Barrier Reef, Australia: **1,400**
- New Caledonia Barrier Reef, South Pacific: **930**
- Mesoamerican Barrier Reef, Caribbean: **620**
- Ningaloo Reef, Western Australia: **162**

Australia's Great Barrier Reef is the only living thing that's clearly visible from space. It stretches along the Queensland coast for 1,400 miles, making it the largest coral reef system in the world. At its northern tip, scientists have discovered a towering, blade-shaped reef, taller than the Empire State Building, that is a mile wide at its base and tapers to a knife edge about 130 feet below the surface. In recent years, climate change has posed a huge threat to the world's coral reefs, with rising sea temperatures causing areas to die off. The northern half of the Great Barrier Reef suffered particularly in 2016, and scientists fear that more damage is yet to come.

167

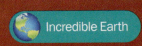 Incredible Earth

world's largest hot desert
SAHARA DESERT

Sahara means simply "great desert," and great it is: It is the largest hot desert on the planet. It's almost the same size as the United States or China and dominates North Africa from the Atlantic Ocean in the west to the Red Sea in the east. It's extremely dry, with most of the Sahara receiving less than 0.1 inches of rain a year, and some places none at all for several years. It is stiflingly hot, up to 122°F, making it one of the hottest and driest regions in the world.

WORLD'S LARGEST HOT DESERTS
Size in square miles

- Sahara Desert, North Africa
- Arabian Desert, Western Asia
- Great Victoria Desert, Australia
- Kalahari Desert, Africa
- Syrian Desert, Western Asia

190,000 • 250,000 • 3.63 million • 220,000 • 900,000

world's largest lake
CASPIAN SEA

Russia, Kazakhstan, Turkmenistan, Iran, and Azerbaijan border the vast Caspian Sea, the largest inland body of water on Earth. Once part of an ancient sea, the lake became landlocked between five and ten million years ago, with occasional fills of salt water as sea levels fluctuated over time. Now it has a surface area of about 149,200 square miles and is home to one of the world's most valuable fish: the beluga sturgeon, the source of beluga caviar, which costs up to $2,250 per pound.

WORLD'S LARGEST LAKES
Area in square miles

- Caspian Sea, Europe/Asia
- Lake Superior, North America
- Lake Victoria, Africa
- Lake Huron, North America
- Lake Michigan, North America

149,200

31,700

26,600

23,000

22,300

Incredible Earth

world's longest river
NILE RIVER

People who study rivers cannot agree on the Nile's source—nobody knows where it actually starts. Some say the most likely source is the Kagera River in Burundi, which is the farthest headstream (a stream that is the source of a river) to flow into Lake Victoria. From the lake, the Nile proper heads north across eastern Africa for 4,132 miles to the Mediterranean. Its water is crucial to people living along its banks. They use it to irrigate precious crops, generate electricity, and, in the lower reaches, as a river highway.

WORLD'S LONGEST RIVERS
Length in miles

- Nile River, Africa — 4,132
- Amazon River, South America — 4,000
- Yangtze River, China — 3,915
- Mississippi–Missouri river system, US — 3,710
- Yellow River, China — 3,395

170

tallest wave ever surfed by a woman
NAZARÉ

The world's tallest surfable waves break on the Portuguese coast at Nazaré, some up to 80 feet tall. It's the place where serious surfers hang out and, in February 2020, Brazilian surfer Maya Gabeira rode a wave 73.5 feet tall. It was the highest wave of the 2019–2020 winter surf season, although Gabeira almost didn't get the chance. In 2013, she was knocked unconscious by a wipeout at Nazaré, and was found facedown in the water with leg and back injuries. After three operations to mend her broken body, she survived and is now a champion!

> **STORM . . . IOTA?**
> Worst-ever Atlantic hurricane season

The year 2020 was stormy, with a record-breaking thirty named storms of tropical-storm strength or higher during the Atlantic hurricane season, from June 1 to November 30. An average season has only twelve or thirteen named storms, but 2020 had fourteen hurricanes alone, the first (Arthur) occurring before the start of the season. Because storms are named alphabetically, this high number meant that meteorologists ran out of letters in the English alphabet and had to name nine storms of the year using the Greek alphabet.

Weather trending

January 2020 is officially the hottest January in the 141 years that we've been recording, according to the US National Oceanic and Atmospheric Administration. Their calculations show that the global land and ocean surface temperature for January 2020 was 2.05 degrees Fahrenheit above the twentieth-century average. The top ten warmest Januarys have all occurred since 2002, and scientists believe that greenhouse gas emissions are largely responsible.

> **GLOBAL WARMING**
> Hottest January in history

FACEBOOK FUNDRAISER
Millions raised for wildfire relief

The year 2020 saw the largest-ever Facebook fundraiser, with more than 1.3 million people around the world donating. The cause was the Australian wildfires relief effort, with donations going to the Trustee for New South Wales Rural Fire Service & Brigades Donations Fund. The drive raised more than US$35 million. The fire service plans to spend US$11.5 million on upgrading safety equipment and US$15 million upgrading local brigades.

LAKE EERIE
Like a scene from Frozen

Homeowners at Lake Erie, in Hamburg, New York, had their lakeside properties turned into ice sculptures in early 2020, after two days of gale-force winds. Photographs showed houses encased in three feet of ice, with dramatic icicle spikes, caused by lake water being buffeted ashore and then freezing solid. Ice-covered windows left homes dark inside, and some residents had to chip their way out of their front doors.

PAYING UP
Billion-dollar disasters

The growing cost of climate change was made apparent in 2020, as the US broke a record for the number of billion-dollar climate disasters. According to the National Oceanic and Atmospheric Administration, the year saw twenty-two disasters costing more than a billion dollars each. Extreme weather played a key role in these events. Droughts and wildfires in the west both made the list, but the majority of the most costly events were hurricanes, tornadoes, and storms in the south and east of the US.

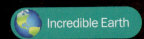 Incredible Earth

most-devastating wildfire season
CALIFORNIA GIGAFIRES

In August 2020 in California, a seasonal drought combined with days of hot weather to dry out leaves, bark, and twigs, transforming them into a powerful fuel. The flashpoint was reached when a series of intense thunderstorms swept through Northern California. Lightning strikes ignited thirty-seven known wildfires, and these grew together, creating the August Complex Fire, California's first "gigafire," which laid waste to more than one million acres across seven counties, an area larger than Rhode Island. In the San Francisco Bay area, the sky glowed orange, and millions of people faced health risks from the thick smoke that enveloped the state and its neighbors.

TOTAL STATS FOR 2020 CALIFORNIA WILDFIRES

75 mph Top speed of the winds that fanned the flames

4.258 million acres The total area damaged by blazes

9,917 Total number of reported fires

10,488 Total number of structures or buildings damaged or destroyed

CLIMATE CHANGE WORRIES
According to climate analysts, out-of-control wildfires have become twice as common in the western United States, and fire seasons are lasting a good three months longer than they did in the 1970s. Climate change has made local conditions hotter and drier, perfect for the rapid spread of wildfires.

Incredible Earth

hottest year on record
2016

Continuing a long-term warming trend, 2020 as good as matched 2016 for being the warmest year since records began in 1880. In 2016, global average temperatures were 1.78°F warmer than they were in the mid-twentieth century, and it was the third year in a row that global temperature records were broken. According to NASA, 2020 was cooler than 2016 by a small fraction of a degree. Most scientists agree that the rising temperatures are caused by a rise in the greenhouse gas carbon dioxide and other human-made emissions in the atmosphere.

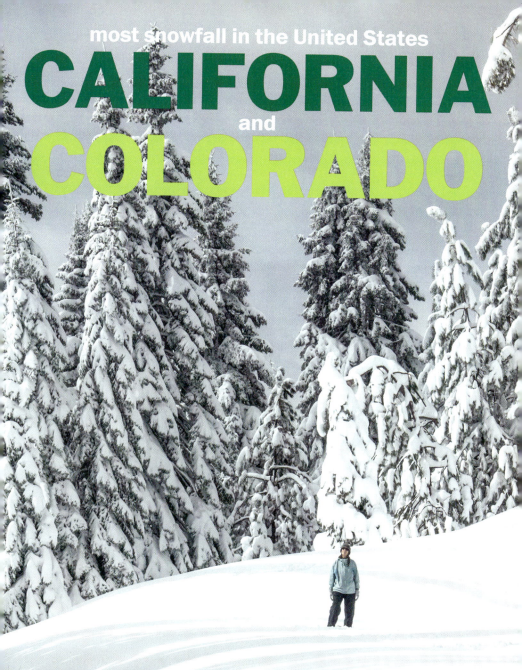

most snowfall in the United States
CALIFORNIA
and
COLORADO

The greatest depth of snow on record in the US occurred at Tamarack, near the Bear Valley ski resort in California, on March 11, 1911. The snow reached an incredible 37.8 feet deep. Tamarack also holds the record for the most snowfall in a single month, with 32.5 feet in January 1911. Mount Shasta, California, had the most snowfall in a single storm with 15.75 feet falling from February 13–19, 1959. The most snow in twenty-four hours was a snowfall of 6.3 feet at Silver Lake, Colorado, on April 14–15, 1921.

The Arctic's record high
VERKHOYANSK,
Siberia

On Saturday June 20, 2020, the Arctic recorded its highest-ever summer temperature when the mercury soared to 100.4°F at Verkhoyansk, a small town in Siberia with weather records dating to 1885. This temperature was 32°F above the monthly average. It came at a time when many out-of-control wildfires coincided with a spate of unusually high temperatures in the Russian Arctic. The town has also been one of the coldest places in the Arctic, with a recorded winter temperature of minus 90°F, which means its inhabitants experience the greatest temperature range anywhere on Earth.

longest lightning bolt
BRAZIL

In June 2020, the World Meteorological Organization (WMO) announced the world's longest lightning bolt, which they discovered by scanning satellite imagery. The bolt occurred two years earlier, on October 31, 2018, when a single flash lit up the Brazilian sky. At 441 miles long—the driving distance roughly between Boston and Washington, DC—the lightning bolt was more than double the length of the previous record holder, a 199.7-mile flash in Oklahoma on June 20, 2007.

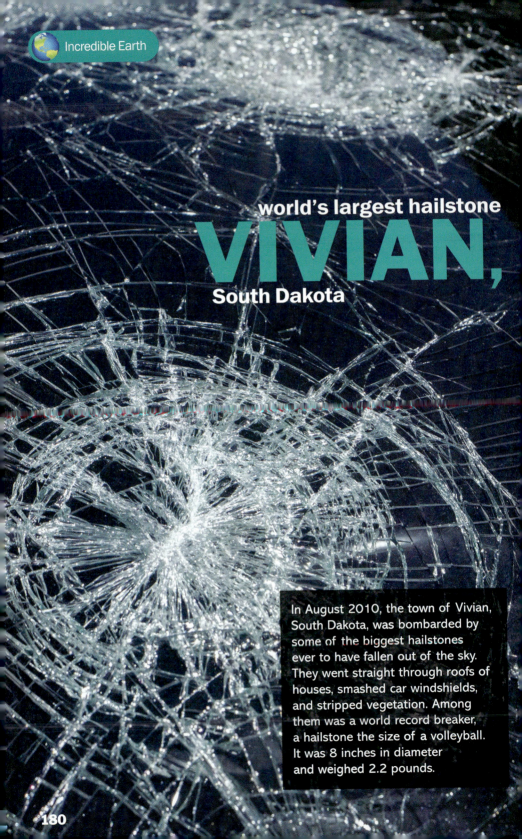

Incredible Earth

world's largest hailstone
VIVIAN,
South Dakota

In August 2010, the town of Vivian, South Dakota, was bombarded by some of the biggest hailstones ever to have fallen out of the sky. They went straight through roofs of houses, smashed car windshields, and stripped vegetation. Among them was a world record breaker, a hailstone the size of a volleyball. It was 8 inches in diameter and weighed 2.2 pounds.

the world's wettest place
MAWSYNRAM

Mawsynram is a cluster of villages in the Khasi Hills of India. The plateau on which they sit overlooks the vast flatlands of Bangladesh. With 467.4 inches of rain falling each year on average, Mawsynram is considered to be the wettest place on Earth. Life here is not without its problems. Wooden bridges are washed away frequently, so locals build living bridges of knotted and interwoven roots of Indian rubber trees. Some people use a traditional "knup" umbrella in the heavy rains. Woven from reeds, they keep the whole body dry.

STATE STATS

8

 State Stats

trending

HISTORIC FIRSTS
Kamala Harris becomes veep

History was made in 2020 when Joe Biden's election victory made his running mate, Kamala Harris, the first woman to hold the office of vice president of the United States. Harris is of Indian and Jamaican heritage, and is both the first Black and first Asian American to become vice president. But 2020 wasn't the first time Harris broke records—she was also California's first Black and first female attorney general, and only the second Black woman ever elected to the US Senate!

THANK YOU, DOLLY!
Country queen funds the vaccine

Dolly Parton made headlines in April 2020 when she donated $1 million to Vanderbilt University's COVID-19 research department. In November, it was revealed that the country-music icon also helped to fund Moderna's COVID-19 vaccine. In February 2021, lawmakers in Tennessee proposed putting a statue of the singer on the grounds of their state capitol to show their gratitude, but Parton graciously rejected the plans, saying that it wasn't appropriate to put her on a pedestal.

Supreme Court justice Ruth Bader Ginsburg—RBG, to her fans—passed away in September 2020, at the age of eighty-seven. The legal and feminist icon was commemorated online with an outpouring of posts on social media, generating 41 million interactions (likes, comments, or shares) in only two days! Social media users used the hashtag #restinpower and praised RBG's dedication to fighting for justice and equality.

MOURNING AN ICON
RBG is remembered by millions

RESCUE MISSION
Happy ending for Texas turtles

February's winter storm had a catastrophic effect on Texas sea turtles, who found themselves in danger in the freezing waters. After hearing about their plight, army and marine corps veteran Will Bellamy knew he had to save them, so he called in some reinforcements! Thanks to Bellamy, more than 1,100 turtles were rescued from Laguna Madre by around fifty navy pilots, students, and military families in the area, and were allowed to recover in the nearby Naval Air Station Corpus Christi.

SANTA'S LITTLE HELPER
Rocky comes to town

The 2020 Rockefeller Center Christmas tree came with a surprising ornament—a tiny saw-whet owl! The bird was discovered clinging to the tree by workers tasked with moving the giant spruce from Oneonta, NY, to the Big Apple. Aptly named Rocky, the owl was taken in by Ravensbeard Wildlife Center, which helped look after the stowaway after she had traveled for three days with no food or water. The pictures of Rocky wrapped in an orange blanket, shared by the center, were the perfect holiday gift for all!

State Stats

ALABAMA

state with the oldest Mardi Gras celebration

French settlers held the first American Mardi Gras in Mobile, Alabama, in 1703. Yearly celebrations continued until the Civil War and began again in 1866. Today, 800,000 people gather in the city during the vibrant two-week festival. Dozens of parades with colorful floats and marching bands wind through the streets each day. Partygoers attend masked balls and other lively events sponsored by the city's social societies. On Mardi Gras, which means "Fat Tuesday" in French, six parades continue the party until the stroke of midnight, which marks the end of the year's festivities and the beginning of Lent.

Native Americans per capita
ALASKA

With a total population of 725,000 people and a Native American population exceeding 145,000, Alaska is the state with the highest number of Native Americans per capita—approximately one in five. Alaska is also the state with the highest number of tribal areas, having more than 200 Native villages in total. Among the great indigenous tribes of Alaska are the Aleut, the Yup'ik, the Eyak, and the Inuit. While most live in modern communities, each continues to uphold the traditions of their elders.

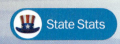 State Stats

state with the best-preserved meteor crater
ARIZONA

Fifty thousand years ago, a meteor traveling at 26,000 miles per hour struck the earth near present-day Winslow, Arizona, to create a mile-wide, 550-foot-deep crater. Today, Meteor Crater is a popular tourist destination and is overseen by stewards who work to educate visitors about its formation. The crater is sometimes known as the Barringer Crater, in recognition of mining engineer Daniel Moreau Barringer, who was the one to propose that it had been made by a meteorite. Previously, geologists had believed that the crater was a natural landform created over time.

only state where diamonds are mined
ARKANSAS

Crater of Diamonds, near Murfreesboro, Arkansas, is the only active public diamond mine in the United States. Farmer and former owner John Wesley Huddleston first discovered diamonds there in August 1906, and a diamond rush overwhelmed the area after he sold the property to a mining company. For a time, there were two competing mines in this area, but in 1969, General Earth Minerals bought both mines to run them as private tourist attractions. Since 1972, the land has been owned by the state of Arkansas, which designated the area as Crater of Diamonds State Park. Visitors can pay a fee to search through plowed fields in the hope of discovering a gem for themselves.

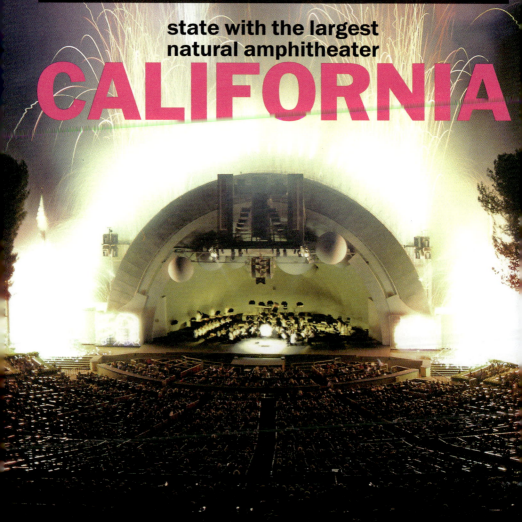

 State Stats

Almost one hundred years since it first opened its doors to the public, the Los Angeles Hollywood Bowl remains the largest natural outdoor amphitheater in the country. The summer home of both the Los Angeles Philharmonic and the Hollywood Bowl Orchestra has a capacity for approximately 17,000 people. Many bring picnics and blankets to make the most of their music-filled summer evenings under the stars. Several events have drawn record crowds, including The Beatles, who attracted 18,700 fans in 1964, and Chris Tomlin, whose 2019 performance was a sellout. The highest attendance record of all time goes to the French singer Lily Pons, whose 1936 performance drew an incredible 26,410 people.

state with the largest natural amphitheater
CALIFORNIA

state with the largest elk population
COLORADO

Colorado is currently home to around 280,000 elk, making it the state with the largest elk population. Elk live on both public and private land across the state, from the mountainous regions to lower terrain. Popular targets for hunting, these creatures are regulated by both the Colorado Parks and Wildlife department and the National Park Service. Many elk live within the boundaries of Colorado's Rocky Mountain National Park. Elk are among the largest members of the deer family, and the males—called bulls—are distinguishable by their majestic antlers.

State Stats

only state to manufacture PEZ candy
CONNECTICUT

The PEZ factory in Orange, Connecticut, is the only place in the United States to make the world-famous candy. In 1927, an Austrian named Eduard Haas III invented PEZ as a breath mint. The letters come from the German word for peppermint, *pfefferminz* (PfeffErminZ). The candy came to the United States in 1952, and the company opened its US factory in 1975. Today, Americans consume an incredible three billion PEZ candies per year. The visitor center in Orange displays the largest collection of PEZ memorabilia on public display in the world, including the world's largest dispenser and a PEZ motorcycle.

state with the most horseshoe crabs
DELAWARE

Delaware Bay has the largest American horseshoe crab (*Limulus polyphemus*) population in the world. These creatures can be seen in large numbers on the bay's beaches in the spring. They appear during high tides on new and full moons when they come onto land to spawn (deposit eggs). Horseshoe crabs have changed very little in the past 250 million years, and have therefore been called "living fossils." It is impossible to know the exact number of horseshoe crabs in the region, so every spring, volunteers at some of the state's beaches conduct counts to track spawning activity. A full survey was not possible in 2020, owing to COVID-19, but in 2019, the Delaware Center for the Inland Bays estimated a record seasonal count of 2,105,447 horseshoe crabs on its beaches.

State Stats

FLORIDA

only state in which alligators and crocodiles live side by side

Where else but Everglades National Park might you expect to see both alligators and crocodiles living in the wild? The alligator is the more common of the two in America. According to the Florida tourist office, "If you don't see one during an Everglades visit, you're doing something wrong." The American crocodile is endangered, and so a rarer find. Both species like to bask in the sun on the banks of mangrove swamps and other bodies of water. The best way to tell the difference between the two is to check the shape of the snout. An alligator has a more U-shaped snout; a crocodile's is shaped more like a V. And did you know? Not only is Florida the only state where you can see alligators and crocodiles, it's also the only place in the world!

194

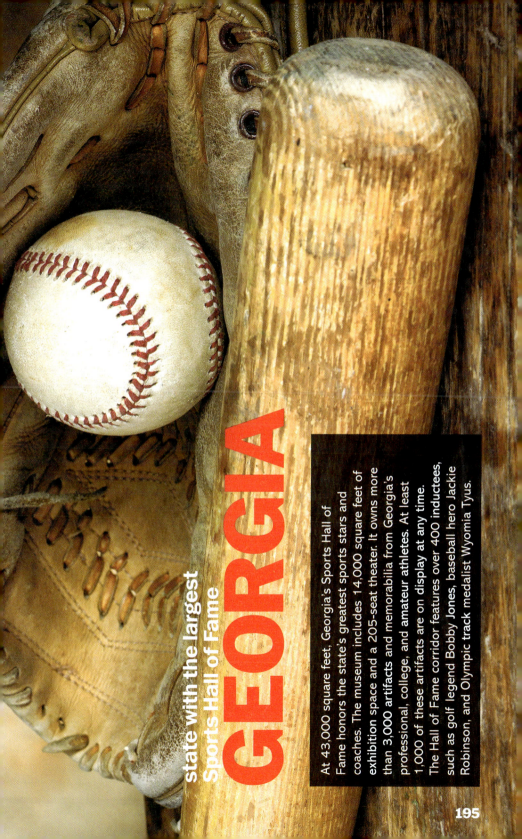

GEORGIA

state with the largest Sports Hall of Fame

At 43,000 square feet, Georgia's Sports Hall of Fame honors the state's greatest sports stars and coaches. The museum includes 14,000 square feet of exhibition space and a 205-seat theater. It owns more than 3,000 artifacts and memorabilia from Georgia's professional, college, and amateur athletes. At least 1,000 of these artifacts are on display at any time. The Hall of Fame corridor features over 400 inductees, such as golf legend Bobby Jones, baseball hero Jackie Robinson, and Olympic track medalist Wyomia Tyus.

State Stats

only state with a royal palace
HAWAII

Iolani Palace, in downtown Honolulu, is the only official royal residence in the United States. The palace was built from 1879–1882 by King Kalakaua, inspired by the styles of the grand castles of Europe. The monarchs did not live there for long, however: In 1893, the kingdom of Hawaii was overthrown by US forces.

Kalakaua's sister, Queen Liliuokalani, was even held prisoner in the palace in 1895 following a plot to put her back on the throne. Iolani Palace was used as a government building until it became a National Historic Landmark in 1962. Restored to its nineteenth-century condition, it is now open to the public as a museum.

first state with a blue football field
IDAHO

Boise State's Albertsons Stadium, originally dubbed the "Smurf Turf" and now nicknamed "The Blue," was the first blue football field in the United States. In 1986, when the time came to upgrade the old turf, athletics director Gene Bleymaier realized that they would be spending a lot of money on the new field, yet most spectators wouldn't notice the difference. So, he asked AstroTurf to create the new field in the school's colors. Since the field's creation, students at the school have consistently voted for blue turf each time the field has been upgraded. Today, nine teams play on a colored playing field, including the Coastal Carolina Chanticleers whose teal field is dubbed "The Surf Turf."

State Stats

state with the oldest free public zoo
ILLINOIS

Lincoln Park Zoo, in Chicago, Illinois, remains the oldest free public zoo in the United States. Founded back in 1868—just nine years after the Philadelphia Zoo, the country's oldest zoo overall—Lincoln Park Zoo does not charge admission fees. More than two-thirds of the money for the zoo's operating budget comes from food, retail, parking, and fund-raising events. Nonetheless, the zoo continues to grow. In November 2016, it opened a new exhibit—the Walter Family Arctic Tundra—to house its newest addition: a seven-year-old male polar bear named Siku.

the first professional baseball game
INDIANA

On May 4, 1871, the first National Association professional baseball game took place on Hamilton Field in Fort Wayne, Indiana. The home team, the Kekiongas, took on the Forest Citys of Cleveland, beating them 2–0 against the odds. The Kekiongas were a little-known team at the time. In fact, the first professional game had been scheduled to take place between two better-known teams, the Washington Olympics and the Cincinnati Red Stockings in Washington, DC, on May 3. Heavy rain forced a cancellation, however, and so history was made at Fort Wayne the following day.

State Stats

At only 296 feet long, Fenelon Place Elevator in Dubuque, Iowa, is the shortest railroad in the United States, and its elevation of 189 feet also makes it the steepest. The original railway was built in 1882 by businessman and former mayor J. K. Graves, who lived at the top of the Mississippi River bluff and wanted a quicker commute down into the town below. Today's railway, modernized in 1977, is open to the public. It costs $1.50 for an **adult** one-way trip and consists of **two** quaint house-shaped cars traveling in opposite directions on parallel tracks.

state with the shortest, steepest railroad
IOWA

state with the most rock concretions
KANSAS

Rock City, in Minneapolis, Kansas, boasts two hundred concretions of Dakota sandstone across a 5-acre park. They are the largest concretions in one place anywhere in the world. These concretions are huge spheres of rock, some of which measure up to 27 feet in diameter. They were created underground millions of years ago, when minerals deposited by water gradually formed hard, strong shells around small bits of matter in the sandstone. Over time, as the surrounding sandstone wore down, the concretions survived. Today, Rock City is a registered National Natural Landmark, and visitors can explore the park and climb the concretions for a $3.00 fee.

 State Stats

state with the biggest fireworks display
KENTUCKY

The Kentucky Derby is the longest-running sporting event in the United States. It's also accompanied by the biggest fireworks display held annually in the United States—"Thunder Over Louisville"—which kicks off the racing festivities. Zambelli Fireworks, the display's creator, says that the show requires nearly 60 tons of fireworks shells and a massive 700 miles of wire cable to sync the fireworks to music. In recent years, the display has fallen foul of COVID-19. Canceled in 2020, the fireworks went ahead in 2021, but did so without spectators, and were televised instead.

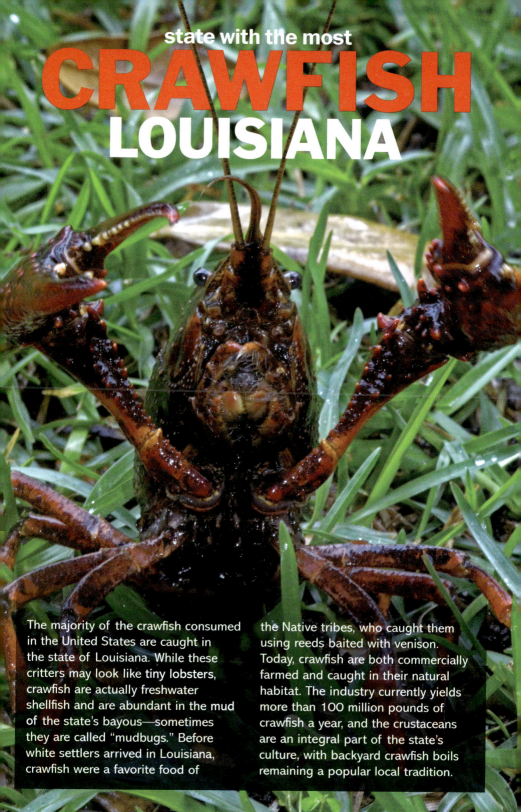

state with the most
CRAWFISH
LOUISIANA

The majority of the crawfish consumed in the United States are caught in the state of Louisiana. While these critters may look like tiny lobsters, crawfish are actually freshwater shellfish and are abundant in the mud of the state's bayous—sometimes they are called "mudbugs." Before white settlers arrived in Louisiana, crawfish were a favorite food of the Native tribes, who caught them using reeds baited with venison. Today, crawfish are both commercially farmed and caught in their natural habitat. The industry currently yields more than 100 million pounds of crawfish a year, and the crustaceans are an integral part of the state's culture, with backyard crawfish boils remaining a popular local tradition.

State Stats

state with the oldest state fair

MAINE

In January 1819, the Somerset Central Agricultural Society sponsored the first-ever Skowhegan State Fair. In the 1800s, state fairs were important places for farmers to gather and learn about new agricultural methods and equipment. After Maine became a state in 1820, the fair continued to grow in size and popularity, gaining its official name in 1842. Today, the Skowhegan State Fair welcomes more than 7,000 exhibitors and 100,000 visitors. Enthusiasts can watch events that include livestock competitions, tractor pulling, a demolition derby, and much more during the ten-day show.

state with the oldest capitol building
MARYLAND

The Maryland State House in Annapolis is both the oldest capitol building in continuous legislative use and the only state house once to have been used as the national capitol. The Continental Congress met there from 1783–1784, and it was where George Washington formally resigned as commander in chief of the army following the American Revolution. The current building is the third to be erected on that site, and was actually incomplete when the Continental Congress met there in 1783, despite the cornerstone being laid in 1772. The interior of the building was finished in 1797, but not without tragedy—plasterer Thomas Dance fell to his death while working on the dome in 1793.

OLDEST CAPITOL BUILDINGS IN 2021
Age of building (year work was started)

1722
Maryland: **249 years**

1785
Virginia: **236 years**

1792
New Jersey: **229 years**

1795
Massachusetts: **226 years**

1816
New Hampshire: **205 years**

State Stats

MASSACHUSETTS

state with the oldest
THANKSGIVING
celebration

The first Thanksgiving celebration took place in 1621, in Plymouth, Massachusetts, when the Pilgrims and the Native Wampoanoag people shared a feast. While the celebration became widespread in the Northeast in the late seventeenth century, Thanksgiving was not celebrated nationally until 1863, when magazine editor Sarah Josepha Hale's writings convinced President Abraham Lincoln to make it a national holiday. Today, Plymouth, Massachusetts, holds a weekend-long celebration honoring its history: the America's Hometown Thanksgiving Celebration.

most magical STATE

MICHIGAN

Colon, Michigan, is known as the magic capital of the world. The small town is home to Abbott Magic Company—one of the biggest manufacturers of magic supplies in the United States—as well as an annual magic festival, magicians' walk of fame, and Lakeside Cemetery, in which thirty magicians are buried. The Abbott plant boasts 50,000 square feet dedicated to creating new tricks—from simple silk scarves to custom illusions. It is the only building in the world expressly built for the purpose of making magic.

State Stats

state with the largest MALL
MINNESOTA

The biggest shopping and entertainment center in the United States is the Mall of America® in Bloomington, Minnesota. Spread over 5.4 million square feet with 12,000 parking spaces, it attracts forty million people a year. As well as the 500 retail units, the mall also contains the Nickelodeon Universe indoor amusement park and an aquarium. Minnesota is also considered the birthplace of the modern shopping mall as it is home to Southdale Center in Edina, one of the first malls, which opened in 1956.

only state to hold the International Ballet Competition

MISSISSIPPI

Every four years, Jackson, Mississippi, hosts the USA International Ballet Competition, a two-week Olympic-style event that awards gold, silver, and bronze medals. The competition began in 1964 in Varna, Bulgaria, and rotated among the cities of Varna; Moscow, Russia; and Tokyo, Japan. In June 1979, the competition came to the United States for the first time, and, in 1982, Congress passed a Joint Resolution designating Jackson as the official home of the competition. In addition to medals, dancers vie for cash prizes and the chance to join established ballet companies.

State Stats

It is said that America's first ice cream cone was introduced through chance inspiration at the St. Louis World's Fair in 1904. According to the most popular story, a Syrian salesman named Ernest Hamwi saw that an ice cream vendor had plenty of ice cream but not enough cups and spoons to serve it. Seeing that a neighboring vendor was selling waffle cookies, Hamwi took a cookie and rolled it into a cone for holding ice cream. An immediate success, Hamwi's invention was hailed by vendors as a "cornucopia"—an exotic word for a "cone."

America's first ice cream cone
MISSOURI

210

state with the most *T. rex* specimens
MONTANA

The first *Tyrannosaurus rex* fossil ever found was discovered in Montana—paleontologist Barnum Brown excavated it in the Hell Creek Formation in 1902. Since then, many major *T. rex* finds have been made in Montana—from the "Wankel Rex," discovered in 1988, to "Trix," unearthed in 2013, and "Tufts-Love Rex," discovered in 2016. This last was found about 20 percent intact at the site in the Hell Creek Formation. In recent years a new exhibit named "Dinosaurs Under the Big Sky" has been installed in the Siebel Dinosaur Complex at the Museum of the Rockies in Bozeman, Montana. It is one of the largest and most up-to-date dinosaur exhibits in the world.

State Stats

state with the largest indoor rain forest
NEBRASKA

The Lied Jungle at the Henry Doorly Zoo in Omaha, Nebraska, features three rain forest habitats: one each from South America, Africa, and Asia. At 123,000 square feet, this indoor rain forest is larger than two football fields. It measures 80 feet tall, making it as tall as an eight-story building. The Lied Jungle opened in 1992 and cost $15 million to create. Seven waterfalls rank among its spectacular features. Ninety different animal species live here, including saki monkeys, pygmy hippos, and many reptiles and birds. Exotic plant life includes the African sausage tree, the chocolate tree, and rare orchids. The zoo's other major exhibit—the Desert Dome—is the world's largest indoor desert.

state that produces the most gold
NEVADA

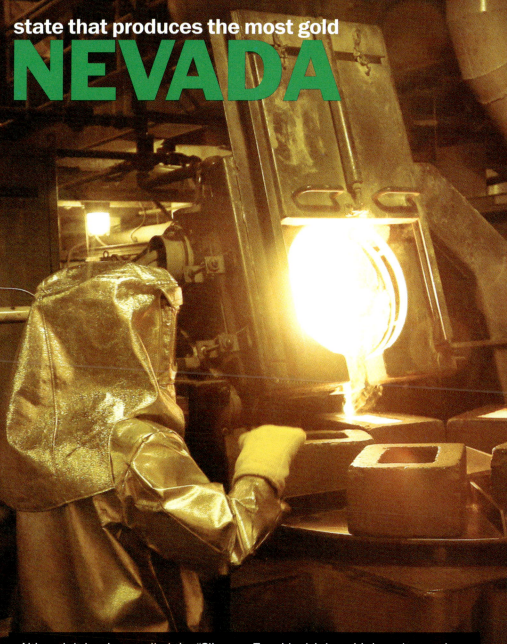

Although it has been called the "Silver State" for its silver production, Nevada is also the state that produces the most gold. According to the Nevada Mining Association, Nevada produces more than three-quarters of America's gold and accounts for 5.4 percent of world gold production. Nevada's Carlin Trend is rich in gold deposits—and is, in fact, the world's second-largest gold resource. In 2020, two new gold deposits were found 20 miles west of Elko in the Ruby Valley. Once production starts, Nevada's gold output could rise by as much as five million ounces of gold over a decade.

NEW HAMPSHIRE

State Stats

state with the oldest skiing club

Nansen Ski Club, in Milan, New Hampshire, was founded by Norwegian immigrants in 1872, making it the oldest continuously operating skiing club in the United States. When it first opened, the venue only accepted other Scandinavians living in the area but was then made available to everyone as more skiing enthusiasts began to move into New Hampshire from Quebec, to work in the mills there. For fifty years, the club was home to the largest ski jump east of the Mississippi, and was used for Olympic tryouts.

214

state with the most diners
NEW JERSEY

The state of New Jersey has more than six hundred diners, earning it the title of "Diner Capital of the World." The state has a higher concentration of diners than anywhere else in the United States. They are such an iconic part of the state's identity that, in 2016, a New Jersey diners exhibit opened at Middlesex County Museum, showcasing the history of the diner from early twentieth-century lunch cars to modern roadside spots. The state has many different types of diners, including famous restaurant-style eateries like Tops in East Newark, as well as retro hole-in-the-wall diners with jukeboxes and faded booths.

State Stats

state that made the world's largest flat enchilada
NEW MEXICO

New Mexico was home to the world's largest flat enchilada in October 2014, during the Whole Enchilada Fiesta in Las Cruces. The record-breaking enchilada measured 10.5 feet in diameter and required 250 pounds of masa dough, 175 pounds of cheese, 75 gallons of red chili sauce, 50 pounds of onions, and 175 gallons of oil. Led by Roberto's Mexican Restaurant, the making—and eating—of the giant enchilada was a tradition at the festival for thirty-four years before enchilada master Roberto Estrada hung up his apron in 2015.

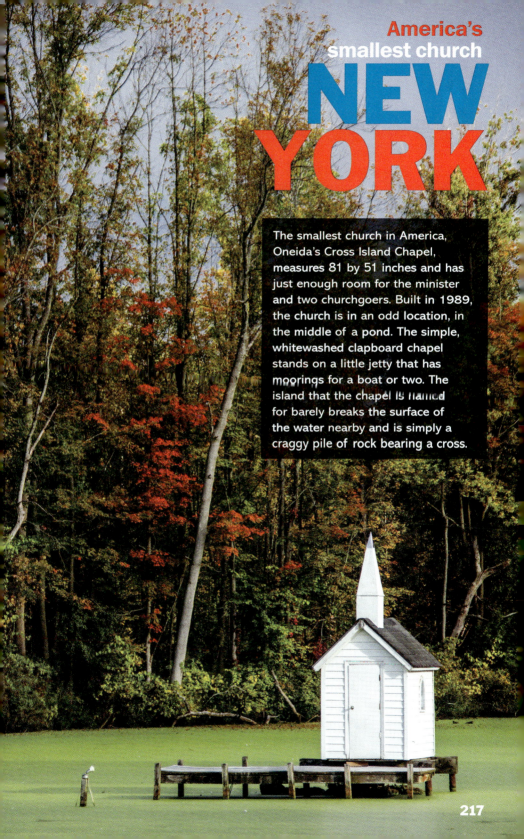

America's smallest church
NEW YORK

The smallest church in America, Oneida's Cross Island Chapel, measures 81 by 51 inches and has just enough room for the minister and two churchgoers. Built in 1989, the church is in an odd location, in the middle of a pond. The simple, whitewashed clapboard chapel stands on a little jetty that has moorings for a boat or two. The island that the chapel is named for barely breaks the surface of the water nearby and is simply a craggy pile of rock bearing a cross.

State Stats

state with the largest private house
NORTH CAROLINA

LARGEST PRIVATE HOUSES IN THE US
Area in square feet

- Biltmore House, Asheville, NC
- Oheka Castle, Huntington, NY
- Sydell Miller Mansion, Palm Beach, FL
- Pensmore, Highlandville, MO
- Rennert Mansion, Sagaponack, NY

 175,000
 109,000
84,626
 72,215
 66,400

The Biltmore Estate, in the mountains of Asheville, North Carolina, is home to Biltmore House, the largest privately owned house in the United States. George Vanderbilt commissioned the 250-room French Renaissance–style chateau in 1889, and opened it to his friends and family as a country retreat in 1895. Designed by architect Richard Morris Hunt, Biltmore House has an impressive thirty-five bedrooms and forty-three bathrooms, and boasts a floor space of over four acres. In 1930, the Vanderbilt family opened Biltmore House to the public.

biggest honey producer
NORTH DAKOTA

For the last fifteen years, North Dakota has outstripped all other US states in the production of honey. Currently, there are 485,000 honey-producing colonies in North Dakota, and in 2018, they produced more than 38.2 million pounds of the sweet stuff. It seems the North Dakota climate is just right for honeybees and—more important—for the flowers from which they collect their nectar. Typical summer weather features warm days but cool nights.

State Stats

first laws protecting
WORKING WOMEN
OHIO

In the 1800s, working conditions in US factories were grueling and pay was very low. Most of the workers were women, and it was not uncommon for them to work for twelve to fourteen hours a day, six days a week. The factories were not heated or air-conditioned and there was no compensation for being sick.

By the 1850s, several organizations had formed to improve the working conditions for women and to shorten their workday. In 1852, Ohio passed a law limiting the working day to ten hours for women under the age of eighteen. It was a small step, but it was also the first act of legislation of its kind in the United States.

state with the largest multiple-arch dam
OKLAHOMA

Completed in 1940, the Pensacola Dam in Oklahoma is 6,565 feet long, making it the longest multiple-arch dam in the world. The dam stretches across the Grand River and controls the 43,500 acres of water that form the Grand Lake o' the Cherokees. The massive structure is a towering 145 feet tall and consists of no fewer than 535,000 cubic yards of concrete, about 655,000 barrels of cement, 75,000 pounds of copper, and a weighty 10 million pounds of structural steel.

State Stats

world's largest cinnamon roll
OREGON

Wolferman's Bakery holds the record for the largest cinnamon roll ever made. The spiced confection measured 9 feet long and was topped with 147 pounds of cream cheese frosting. It was made to celebrate the launch of the bakery's new 5-pound cinnamon roll. Using its popular recipe, Wolferman's needed 20 pounds of eggs, 350 pounds of flour, 378 pounds of cinnamon-sugar filling, and no fewer than 220 cinnamon sticks in their scaled-up version. The 1,150-pound cinnamon roll was transported to Medford's Annual Pear Blossom Festival in south Oregon, where visitors snapped it up for $2 a slice.

state that manufactures the most crayons
PENNSYLVANIA

Easton, Pennsylvania, is home to the Crayola crayon factory and has been the company's headquarters since 1976. The factory produces an amazing twelve million crayons every single day, made from uncolored paraffin and pigment powder. In 1996, the company opened the Crayola Experience in downtown Easton. The Experience includes a live interactive show in which guests can watch a "crayonologist" make crayons, just as they are made at the factory nearby.

223

RHODE ISLAND

state with the oldest Fourth of July celebration

State Stats

Bristol, Rhode Island, holds America's longest continuously running Fourth of July celebration. The idea for the celebration came from Revolutionary War veteran Rev. Henry Wight, of Bristol's First Congregational Church, who organized "Patriotic Exercises" to honor the nation's founders and those who fought to establish the United States. Today, Bristol begins celebrating the holiday on June 14, and puts on a wide array of events leading up to the Fourth itself—including free concerts, a baseball game, a Fourth of July Ball, and a half marathon.

224

state with the hottest
PEPPER
SOUTH CAROLINA

Pepper X, created by Smokin' Ed Currie of Rock Hill, South Carolina, is the hottest pepper in the world, measuring an average of 3.18 million Scoville heat units (SHU). To get a feel for how hot that is, just know that a regular jalapeño clocks in at 2,500 to 8,000 SHU. Currie also created the world's third-hottest chili, the Carolina Reaper®. The Reaper held the record from 2013 to 2017, before being beaten by the 2.4 million SHU Dragon's Breath pepper in May. Just four months after that, Currie's Pepper X took the chili pepper world by storm.

WORLD'S HOTTEST PEPPERS
By peak heat in millions of SHU

- Pepper X
- Dragon's Breath
- Carolina Reaper®
- Trinidad Moruga Scorpion

3.18 2.4 2.2 2

State Stats

state with the largest sculpture
SOUTH DAKOTA

While South Dakota is famous as the home of Mount Rushmore, it is also the location of another giant mountain carving: the Crazy Horse Memorial. The mountain carving, which is still in progress, will be the largest sculpture in the world when it is completed, at 563 feet tall and 641 feet long. Korczak Ziolkowski, who worked on Mount Rushmore, began the carving in 1948 to pay tribute to Crazy Horse—the Lakota leader who defeated General Custer at the Battle of the Little Bighorn. Nearly seventy years later, Ziolkowski's family continues his work, relying completely on funding from visitors and donors.

state that makes all the MoonPies
TENNESSEE

Tennessee is the home of the MoonPie, which was conceived there in 1917 by bakery salesman Earl Mitchell Sr. after a group of local miners asked for a filling treat "as big as the moon." Made from marshmallow, graham crackers, and chocolate, the sandwich cookies were soon being mass-produced at Tennessee's Chattanooga Bakery, and MoonPie was registered as a trademark by the bakery in 1919. MoonPies first sold at just five cents each and quickly became popular—even being named the official snack of NASCAR in the late 1990s. Today, Chattanooga Bakery makes nearly a million MoonPies every day.

 State Stats

largest urban bat colony
TEXAS

If you want to see a sky filled with hundreds of thousands of bats, head to Austin, Texas, any time from mid-March to November. The city's Ann W. Richards Congress Avenue Bridge is home to the world's largest urban bat colony—roughly 1.5 million bats in all. The Mexican free-tailed bats first settled here in the 1980s, and numbers have grown steadily since. They currently produce around 750,000 pups per year. These days the bats are a tourist attraction that draws about 140,000 visitors to the city, many of them hoping to catch the moment at dusk when large numbers of bats fly out from under the bridge to look for food.

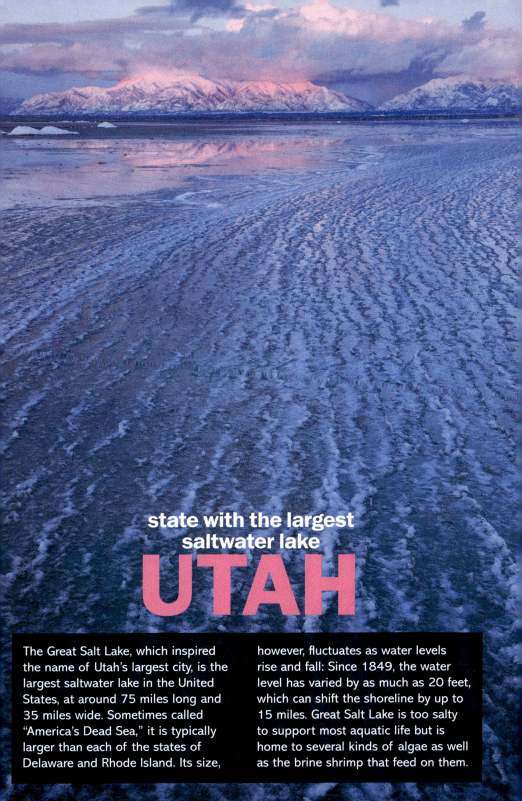

state with the largest saltwater lake
UTAH

The Great Salt Lake, which inspired the name of Utah's largest city, is the largest saltwater lake in the United States, at around 75 miles long and 35 miles wide. Sometimes called "America's Dead Sea," it is typically larger than each of the states of Delaware and Rhode Island. Its size, however, fluctuates as water levels rise and fall: Since 1849, the water level has varied by as much as 20 feet, which can shift the shoreline by up to 15 miles. Great Salt Lake is too salty to support most aquatic life but is home to several kinds of algae as well as the brine shrimp that feed on them.

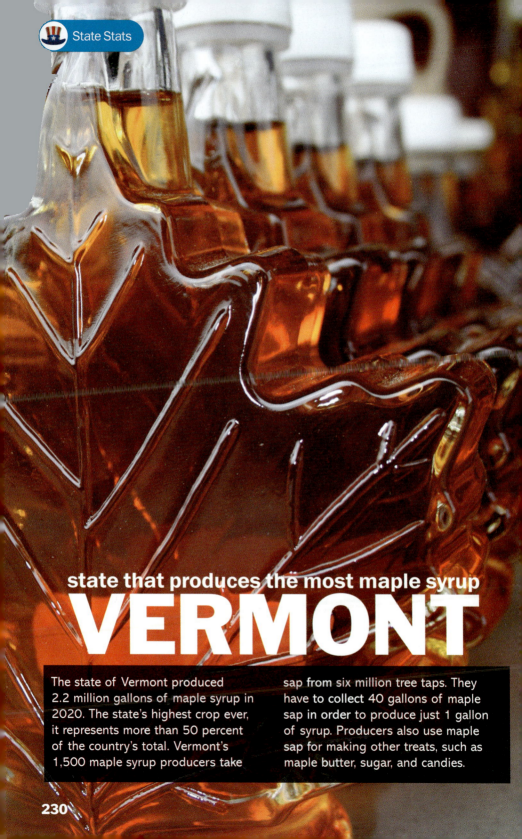

State Stats

state that produces the most maple syrup
VERMONT

The state of Vermont produced 2.2 million gallons of maple syrup in 2020. The state's highest crop ever, it represents more than 50 percent of the country's total. Vermont's 1,500 maple syrup producers take sap from six million tree taps. They have to collect 40 gallons of maple sap in order to produce just 1 gallon of syrup. Producers also use maple sap for making other treats, such as maple butter, sugar, and candies.

The Pentagon—the headquarters of the United States Department of Defense—is America's largest office building. The five-sided structure, which was completed in 1943 after just sixteen months of work, cost $83 million to build. It contains 3.7 million square feet of office space—triple the amount of floor space in the Empire State Building—as well as a large central courtyard. Despite containing 17.5 miles of corridors, the building's design means that a person can walk from any point to another in about seven minutes. There are currently 24,000 employees, both military and civilian, working in the building.

state with the largest office building
VIRGINIA

🎩 State Stats

state with the oldest GAS station
WASHINGTON

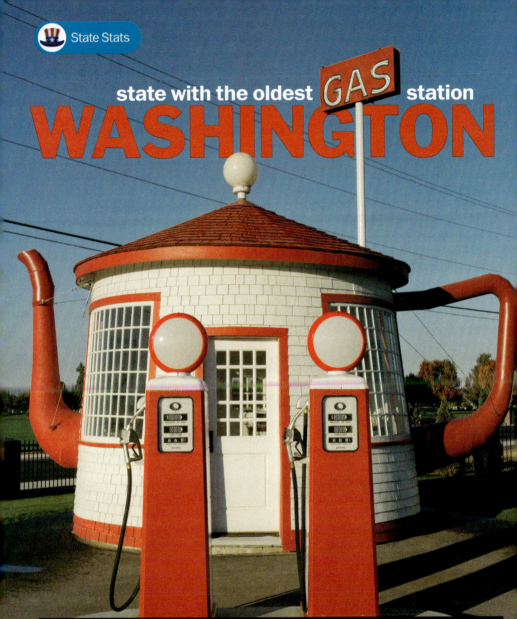

The Teapot Dome Service Station in Zillah, Washington, was once the oldest working gas station in the United States, and is still the only one built to commemorate a political scandal. Now preserved as a museum, the gas station was built in 1922 as a monument to the Teapot Dome Scandal, in which Albert Fall, President Warren G. Harding's secretary of the interior, took bribes to lease government oil reserves to private companies. The gas station, located on Washington's Old Highway 12, was moved in 1978 to make way for Interstate 82, then again in 2007 when it was purchased by the City of Zillah as a historic landmark.

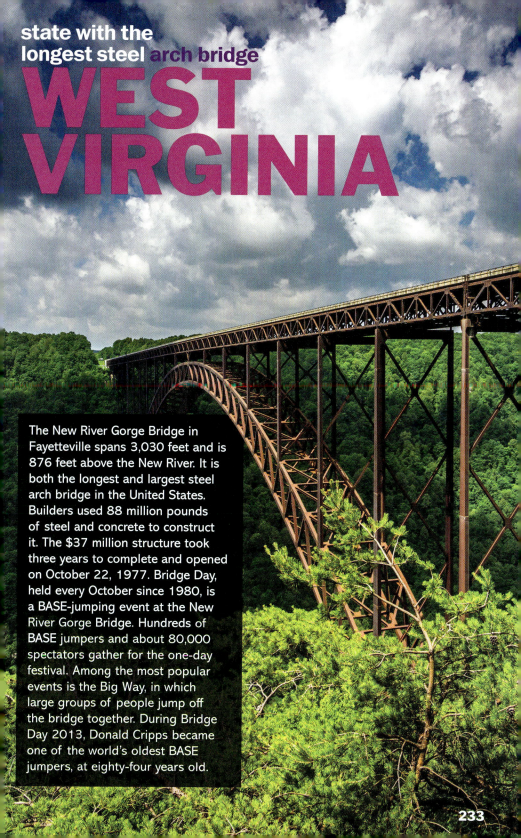

state with the longest steel arch bridge
WEST VIRGINIA

The New River Gorge Bridge in Fayetteville spans 3,030 feet and is 876 feet above the New River. It is both the longest and largest steel arch bridge in the United States. Builders used 88 million pounds of steel and concrete to construct it. The $37 million structure took three years to complete and opened on October 22, 1977. Bridge Day, held every October since 1980, is a BASE-jumping event at the New River Gorge Bridge. Hundreds of BASE jumpers and about 80,000 spectators gather for the one-day festival. Among the most popular events is the Big Way, in which large groups of people jump off the bridge together. During Bridge Day 2013, Donald Cripps became one of the world's oldest BASE jumpers, at eighty-four years old.

State Stats

largest cross-country ski race
WISCONSIN

Each year in February, Wisconsin hosts America's largest cross-country ski race. The race attracts over 10,000 skiers, all attempting to complete the 55-kilometer (34-mile) course from Cable to Hayward. Milestones along the way include Boedecker Hill, Mosquito Brook, and Hatchery Park. The event is part of the Worldloppet circuit of twenty ski marathons across the globe. The winner of the 2021 race, Ian Torchia from Rochester, Minnesota, completed the course in two hours, thirty-nine minutes, and one second to claim the $7,500 prize money.

state with the largest hot spring
WYOMING

Grand Prismatic Spring, in Yellowstone National Park in Wyoming, is the largest hot spring in the United States. The spring measures 370 feet in diameter and is more than 121 feet deep; Yellowstone National Park says that the spring is bigger than a football field and deeper than a ten-story building. Grand Prismatic is not just the largest spring but also the most photographed thermal feature in Yellowstone due to its bright colors. The colors come from different kinds of bacteria, living in each part of the spring, that thrive at various temperatures. As water comes up from the middle of the spring, it is too hot to support most bacterial life, but as the water spreads out to the edges of the spring, it cools in concentric circles.

235

SPORTS STARS

9

A TRAGIC LOSS
Kobe Bryant dies in a helicopter crash

On January 26, Lakers legend Kobe Bryant was killed in a tragic helicopter crash, along with his thirteen-year-old daughter Gianna and seven other passengers. Bryant's passing was mourned by fans around the world, but especially in his home city of Los Angeles, where August 24 was named Kobe Bryant Day in his honor.

 Sports Stars

trending

1080!
Brazilian skateboarder breaks records

Eleven-year-old Gui Khury broke not one, but two Guinness World Records in 2020! Not only was he the youngest athlete to take part in the X Games, an extreme sports contest, but he also became the first skateboarder to land a 1080-degree spin on a vertical ramp. That's three whole rotations of the board! The Brazilian prodigy practiced for this epic feat on a ramp he built in his grandmother's yard during the lockdown.

NATIONAL HERO
Premier League star turns activist

Liverpool Football Club's Marcus Rashford was awarded an MBE (Member of the Most Excellent Order of the British Empire) in 2020, as he became a national hero in England for his activism. Rashford, who grew up getting free school meals, campaigned tirelessly (and successfully) for the program to feed struggling children during the lockdown.

AIRTIME FOR MICHAEL
The Last Dance goes worldwide

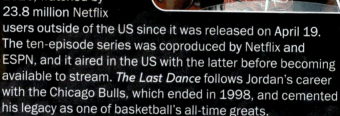

The Michael Jordan docuseries *The Last Dance* went viral in 2020, watched by 23.8 million Netflix users outside of the US since it was released on April 19. The ten-episode series was coproduced by Netflix and ESPN, and it aired in the US with the latter before becoming available to stream. *The Last Dance* follows Jordan's career with the Chicago Bulls, which ended in 1998, and cemented his legacy as one of basketball's all-time greats.

TEAMWORK MAKES THE DREAM WORK
Star-studded ownership group leads NWSL expansion

The US National Women's Soccer League announced a new expansion team in July 2020—the aptly named Angel City FC. This Los Angeles-based franchise has a strong team of women behind the scenes as well as on the field, with a majority-female investing team of businesswomen, celebrities, and sportswomen! The star-studded list of backers includes names such as Natalie Portman, Serena Williams, and Olympic skier Lindsey Vonn.

239

Sports Stars

FRED FUGEN AND VINCE REFFET

world's highest BASE jump from a building

BASE jumping is just about the world's most terrifying sport to watch. BASE stands for the types of places a person may jump from: Buildings, Antennae, Spans (usually bridges), and Earth (usually cliffs). In April 2014, French daredevils Fred Fugen and Vince Reffet set a new record by jumping from a specially built platform at the top of the world's tallest building, the Burj Khalifa in Dubai. They jumped from a height of 2,716 feet, 6 inches. The highest-ever BASE jump was performed by Russian Valery Rozov on a mountain in the Himalayas called Cho Oyu. He jumped from a height of 25,250 feet and landed some 4,450 feet below 3½ minutes later.

EDDIE
ARCARO

Many horse-racing experts think that Eddie Arcaro was the best-ever American jockey. Arcaro rode his first winner in 1932, and by the time of his retirement thirty years later, he had won the Triple Crown twice, in 1941 and 1948. He also won more Triple Crown races than any other jockey, although Bill Hartack has equaled Arcaro's total of five successes in the Kentucky Derby. Arcaro won 4,779 races overall in his career.

JOCKEYS WITH MULTIPLE WINS IN TRIPLE CROWN RACES
Number of wins (years active)

Eddie Arcaro	17	1932–1957
Bill Shoemaker	11	1955–1986
Earl Sande	9	1921–1930
Bill Hartack	9	1956–1969
Pat Day	9	1985–2000
Gary Stevens	9	1988–2013

Sports Stars

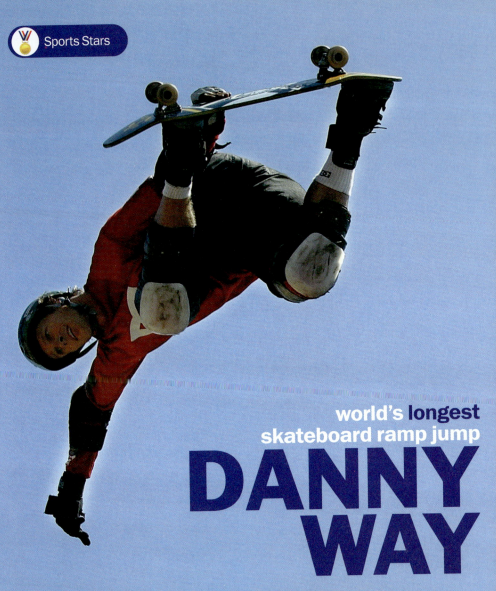

world's longest skateboard ramp jump
DANNY WAY

Many extreme sports activities are showcased at the annual X Games and Winter X Games. At the 2004 X Games, held in Los Angeles, skateboarder Danny Way set an amazing record that remains unbeaten. On June 19, Way made a long-distance jump of 79 feet, beating his own 2003 world record (75 feet). In 2005, he jumped over the Great Wall of China. He made the jump despite having torn ligaments in his ankle during a practice jump on the previous day.

world's highest tightrope walk
FREDDY NOCK

Tightrope walking looks hard enough a few feet above the ground, but Swiss stuntman Freddy Nock took it to the next level when he walked between two mountains in the Swiss Alps in March 2015. On a rope set 11,590 feet above sea level, Freddy took about thirty-nine minutes to walk the 1,140 feet across to the neighboring peak. The previous record had held since 1974, when Frenchman Philippe Petit walked between the Twin Towers of New York's former World Trade Center.

Sports Stars

world's highest basketball shot
HOW RIDICULOUS

Australian trick-shot group How Ridiculous continues to break its own record. In 2015, one member made a basket from an amazing 415 feet, but the group has since improved that distance several times. In January 2018, How Ridiculous achieved its most astonishing feat yet: a basket from 660 feet, 10 inches. The group made the record shot at Maletsunyane Falls, Lesotho, in southern Africa, after five days of setup work and practice. How Ridiculous is a group of three friends who started trying trick shots for fun in their backyards in 2009. They now have a successful YouTube channel and business and are also involved in Christian charitable work.

NBA championships' greatest rivalry
BOSTON CELTICS AND LA LAKERS

NBA CHAMPIONSHIP WINS		
LA Lakers	17	1949–2020
Boston Celtics	17	1957–2008
Golden State Warriors	6	1947–2018
Chicago Bulls	6	1991–1998
San Antonio Spurs	5	1999–2014

Between them, the LA Lakers and Boston Celtics have won almost half of the NBA Championships titles that have ever been played: seventeen each. The Celtics' best decade was the 1960s, when they won nine times, but the Lakers have arguably the better NBA record overall, with fifteen runner-up spots compared to four for the Celtics. There have also been famous player rivalries, that of Larry Bird and Magic Johnson in the 1980s perhaps being the best known.

Sports Stars

NBA MOST CAREER POINTS LEADERS
Number of points

Kareem Abdul-Jabbar	38,387
Karl Malone	36,928
LeBron James	35,236
Kobe Bryant	33,643
Michael Jordan	32,292

most career points in the NBA

KAREEM ABDUL-JABBAR

Many fans regard Kareem Abdul-Jabbar as the greatest-ever basketball player. He was known by his birth name, Lew Alcindor, until 1971, when he changed his name after converting to Islam. That same year he led the Milwaukee Bucks to the team's first NBA championship title. As well as being the all-time highest scorer of points during his professional career with a regular season total of 38,387, Abdul-Jabbar also won the NBA Most Valuable Player (MVP) award a record six times.

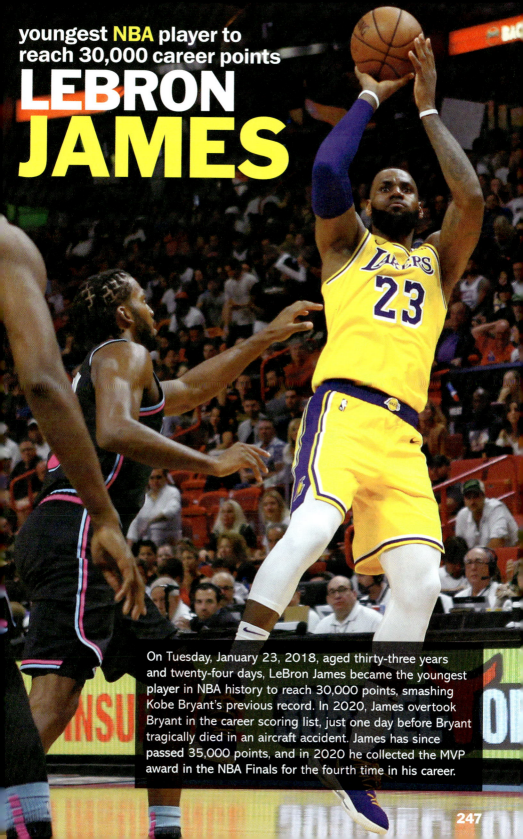

youngest NBA player to reach 30,000 career points
LEBRON JAMES

On Tuesday, January 23, 2018, aged thirty-three years and twenty-four days, LeBron James became the youngest player in NBA history to reach 30,000 points, smashing Kobe Bryant's previous record. In 2020, James overtook Bryant in the career scoring list, just one day before Bryant tragically died in an aircraft accident. James has since passed 35,000 points, and in 2020 he collected the MVP award in the NBA Finals for the fourth time in his career.

Sports Stars

MOST CAREER POINTS IN THE WNBA
Number of points

Diana Taurasi	8,931
Tina Thompson	7,488
Tamika Catchings	7,380
Cappie Pondexter	6,811
Candice Dupree	6,728
Katie Smith	6,452

WNBA player with the most career points

DIANA TAURASI

After a standout college career and three NCAA championships with the University of Connecticut Huskies, Diana Taurasi joined the Phoenix Mercury in the WNBA in 2004. Her prolific scoring helped the Mercury to their first WNBA title in 2007 (and two more since then), and her international career includes four consecutive Team USA Olympic golds, 2004–2016. Playing mainly as guard, Taurasi became the all-time leading WNBA scorer in 2017.

NFL player with the most career touchdowns
JERRY RICE

Jerry Rice is generally regarded as the greatest wide receiver in NFL history. He played in the NFL for twenty seasons—fifteen of them with the San Francisco 49ers—and won three Super Bowl rings. As well as leading the career touchdowns list with 208, Rice also holds the "most yards gained" mark with 23,546 yards. Most of his touchdowns were from pass receptions (197), often working with the great 49ers quarterback Joe Montana.

NFL PLAYERS WITH THE MOST CAREER TOUCHDOWNS
Number of touchdowns (career years)

Jerry Rice	208	1985–2004
Emmitt Smith	175	1990–2004
LaDainian Tomlinson	162	2001–2011
Terrell Owens	156	1996–2010
Randy Moss	156	1998–2012

Sports Stars

NFL player with the most pass completions
DREW BREES

NFL PLAYERS WITH THE MOST PASS COMPLETIONS
Number of completions (career years)

Drew Brees	7,142	2001–2020
Tom Brady	6,778	2000–2020
Brett Favre	6,300	1991–2010
Peyton Manning	6,125	1998–2015
Philip Rivers	5,277	2004–2020

Drew Brees is one of the greatest quarterbacks of all time. After a stellar college career at Purdue, he spent five seasons with the San Diego Chargers before joining the New Orleans Saints in 2006. He was still starring with the Saints in 2018, setting a new season's record for pass completion percentage, which he then nearly beat in 2019. He has now recorded six of the best eight pass completion seasons in NFL history. As well as total pass completions, Brees holds the NFL record for career passing yards. He announced his retirement in March 2021.

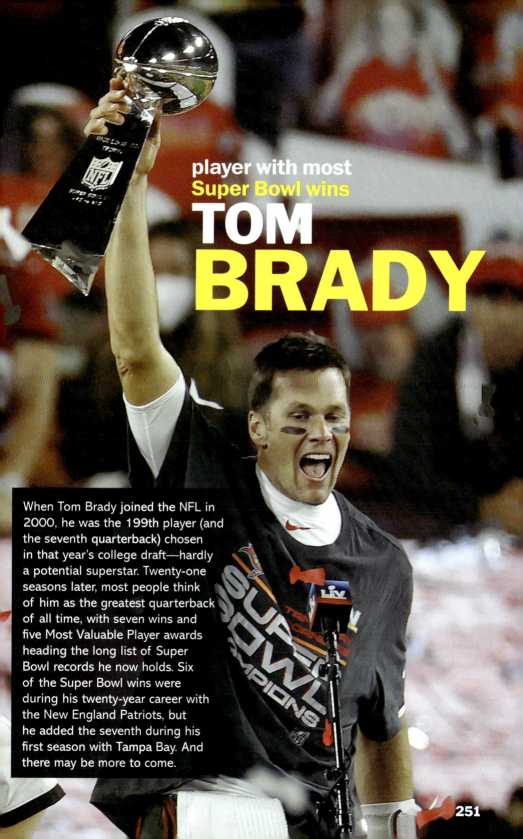

player with most Super Bowl wins
TOM BRADY

When Tom Brady joined the NFL in 2000, he was the 199th player (and the seventh quarterback) chosen in that year's college draft—hardly a potential superstar. Twenty-one seasons later, most people think of him as the greatest quarterback of all time, with seven wins and five Most Valuable Player awards heading the long list of Super Bowl records he now holds. Six of the Super Bowl wins were during his twenty-year career with the New England Patriots, but he added the seventh during his first season with Tampa Bay. And there may be more to come.

Sports Stars

The Rose Bowl is college football's oldest postseason event, first played in 1902. Taking place near January 1 of each year, the game is normally played between the Pac-12 Conference champion and the Big Ten Conference champion, but one year in three it is part of college football's playoffs. The University of Southern California has easily the best record in the Rose Bowl, with twenty-five wins from thirty-four appearances, followed by the Michigan Wolverines (eight wins from twenty). The Alabama Crimson Tide defeated the Fighting Irish of Notre Dame 31–14 on New Year's Day 2021, completing Alabama's eighteenth national championship success.

school with the most Rose Bowl wins
USC
TROJANS

MLB team with the most World Series wins
NEW YORK YANKEES

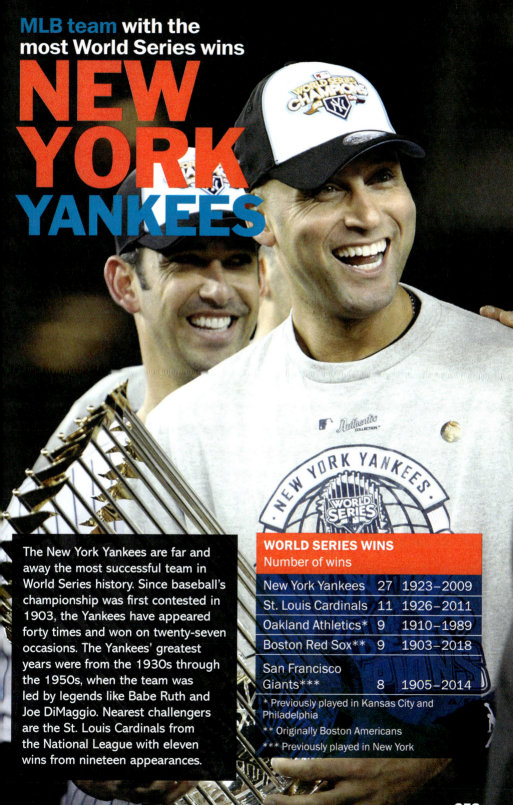

The New York Yankees are far and away the most successful team in World Series history. Since baseball's championship was first contested in 1903, the Yankees have appeared forty times and won on twenty-seven occasions. The Yankees' greatest years were from the 1930s through the 1950s, when the team was led by legends like Babe Ruth and Joe DiMaggio. Nearest challengers are the St. Louis Cardinals from the National League with eleven wins from nineteen appearances.

WORLD SERIES WINS
Number of wins

New York Yankees	27	1923–2009
St. Louis Cardinals	11	1926–2011
Oakland Athletics*	9	1910–1989
Boston Red Sox**	9	1903–2018
San Francisco Giants***	8	1905–2014

* Previously played in Kansas City and Philadelphia
** Originally Boston Americans
*** Previously played in New York

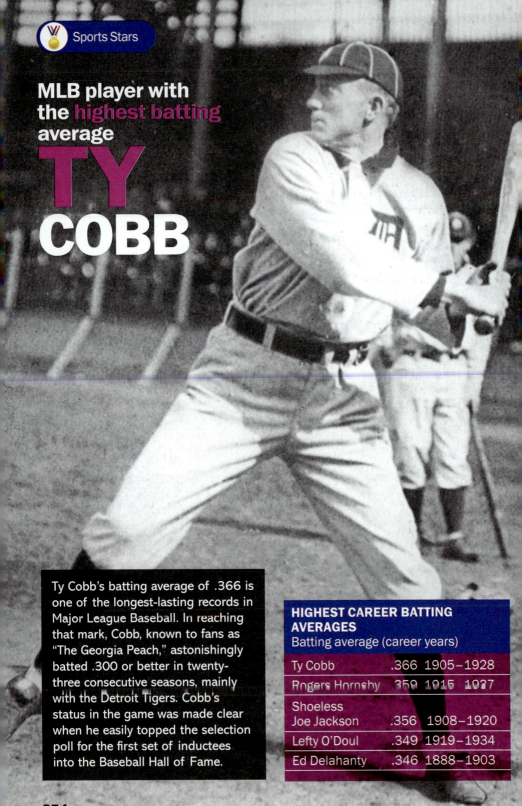

Sports Stars

MLB player with the highest batting average
TY COBB

Ty Cobb's batting average of .366 is one of the longest-lasting records in Major League Baseball. In reaching that mark, Cobb, known to fans as "The Georgia Peach," astonishingly batted .300 or better in twenty-three consecutive seasons, mainly with the Detroit Tigers. Cobb's status in the game was made clear when he easily topped the selection poll for the first set of inductees into the Baseball Hall of Fame.

HIGHEST CAREER BATTING AVERAGES
Batting average (career years)

Ty Cobb	.366	1905–1928
Rogers Hornsby	.359	1915–1937
Shoeless Joe Jackson	.356	1908–1920
Lefty O'Doul	.349	1919–1934
Ed Delahanty	.346	1888–1903

MLB player with the most home runs
BARRY BONDS

Barry Bonds's power hitting and skill in the outfield rank him as a five-tool player—someone with good speed and baserunning skills, who is also good at hitting the ball, fielding, and throwing. He played his first seven seasons with the Pittsburgh Pirates before moving to the San Francisco Giants for the next twelve seasons. He not only holds the record for most career home runs, but also for the single-season record of seventy-three home runs, which was set in 2001. Barry's godfather is Willie Mays, the first player ever to hit 300 career home runs and steal 300 bases.

CAREER HOME RUNS
Number of home runs (career years)

Barry Bonds	762	1986–2007
Hank Aaron	755	1954–1976
Babe Ruth	714	1914–1935
Alex Rodriguez	696	1994–2016
Albert Pujols	662	2001–

Sports Stars

MLS REGULAR-SEASON TOP SCORERS
Number of goals (career years)

Chris Wondolowski	166	2005–
Landon Donovan	145	2001–2016
Jeff Cunningham	134	1998–2011
Jaime Moreno	133	1996–2010
Kei Kamara	130	2006–

Californian Chris Wondolowski took a while to get his professional soccer career going. He was drafted by the San Jose Earthquakes in a late round in 2005 but didn't earn a regular starting spot with the Quakes until 2010. Since then, however, he has scored more than ten goals for San Jose every season up to 2019. He added seven more to his total in the COVID-affected 2020 season but has announced that 2021 will be his last year. He has also earned thirty-five appearances for the US Men's National Team.

MLS player with the most regular-season goals

CHRIS WONDOLOWSKI

country with the most FIFA World Cup wins
BRAZIL

Brazil, host of the 2014 FIFA World Cup, has lifted the trophy the most times in the tournament's history. Second on the list, Germany, has more runners-up and semifinal appearances and hence, arguably, a stronger record overall. However, many would say that Brazil's 1970 lineup, led by the incomparable Pelé, ranks as the finest team ever. The host team has won five of the twenty tournaments that have been completed to date.

FIFA WORLD CUP WINNERS
Number of wins

Brazil	5	1958, 1962, 1970, 1994, 2002
Germany*	4	1954, 1974, 1990, 2014
Italy	4	1934, 1938, 1982, 2006
Uruguay	2	1930, 1950
Argentina	2	1978, 1986
France	2	1998, 2018

* As West Germany 1954, 1974

Sports Stars

FIFA WOMEN'S WORLD CUP WINNERS
Number of wins

United States	4	1991, 1999, 2015, 2019
Germany	2	2003, 2007
Norway	1	1995
Japan	1	2011

country with the most FIFA Women's World Cup wins

UNITED STATES

In 1991, the first Women's World Cup was held, in which the USA beat Norway 2–1 in the final. Since then, the United States has won the tournament three times more. Megan Rapinoe was named the best player of the tournament following the USA's 2019 triumph. She scored the team's second goal in the 2–0 victory over the Netherlands in the final.

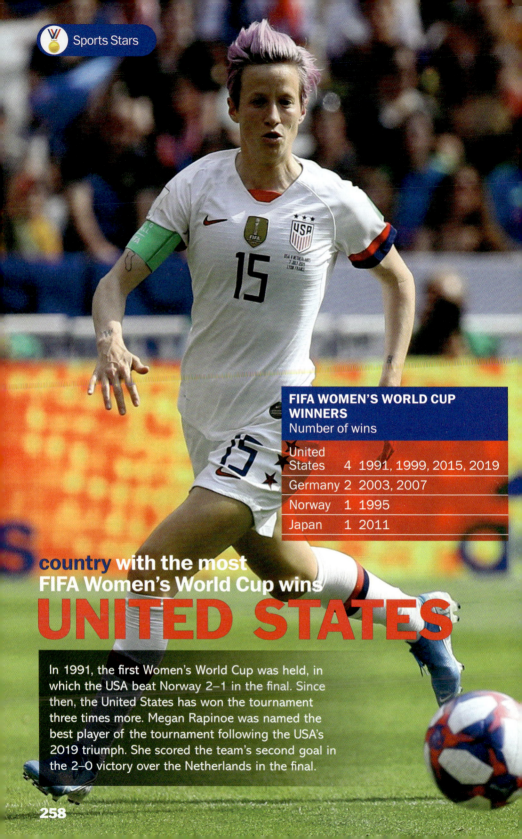

woman with the most international soccer caps

KRISTINE LILLY

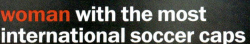

In her long and successful career, Kristine Lilly played club soccer principally with the Boston Breakers. When she made her debut on the US national team in 1987, however, she was still in high school. Her total of 354 international caps is the world's highest for a man or woman, and her trophy haul includes two World Cup winner's medals and two Olympic golds.

WOMEN WITH THE MOST INTERNATIONAL SOCCER CAPS
Number of caps (career years)

Kristine Lilly, USA	354	1987–2010
Christie Pearce, USA	311	1997–2015
Carli Lloyd, USA	300	2005–
Christine Sinclair, Canada	296	2000–
Mia Hamm, USA	276	1987–2004

Sports Stars

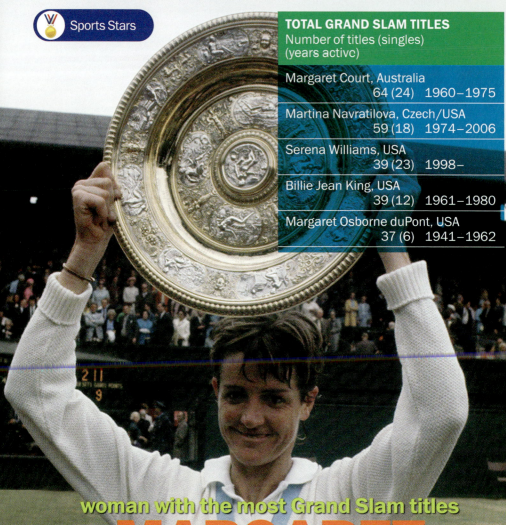

TOTAL GRAND SLAM TITLES
Number of titles (singles)
(years active)

Margaret Court, Australia	64 (24)	1960–1975
Martina Navratilova, Czech/USA	59 (18)	1974–2006
Serena Williams, USA	39 (23)	1998–
Billie Jean King, USA	39 (12)	1961–1980
Margaret Osborne duPont, USA	37 (6)	1941–1962

woman with the most Grand Slam titles
MARGARET COURT

The Grand Slam tournaments are the four most important tennis events of the year: the Australian Open, the French Open, Wimbledon, and the US Open. The dominant force in women's tennis throughout the 1960s and into the 1970s, Australia's Margaret Court heads the all-time singles list with twenty-four, although Serena Williams may beat this. Court won an amazing sixty-four Grand Slam titles in singles, women's doubles, and mixed doubles, a total that seems unlikely to be beaten.

men with the most Grand Slam singles titles

ROGER FEDERER, RAFAEL NADAL, AND NOVAK DJOKOVIC

GRAND SLAM SINGLES WINS Number of wins (years active)		
Roger Federer, Switzerland	20	1998–
Rafael Nadal, Spain	20	2001–
Novak Djokovic, Serbia	19	2003–
Pete Sampras, USA	14	1988–2002
Roy Emerson, Australia	12	1961–1973

Between 2003 and early 2021, seventy-one Grand Slam tennis tournaments were held, and these three great players—Roger Federer, Rafael Nadal, and Novak Djokovic—won fifty-nine of them. Their domination was clearest during 2005–2009 when they collectively won eighteen consecutive Grand Slams among them. Federer notched the trio's first success at Wimbledon in 2003 and may now finally have passed his best years, but Nadal won in France in 2020 and Djokovic in France and Australia in 2021.

 Sports Stars

most consecutive NASCAR championship wins
JIMMIE JOHNSON

NASCAR CHAMPIONSHIP WINS
Number of wins (years in which the title was won)

Jimmie Johnson	7	2006, 2007, 2008, 2009, 2010, 2013, 2016
Dale Earnhardt Sr.	7	1980, 1986, 1987, 1990, 1991, 1993, 1994
Richard Petty	7	1964, 1967, 1971, 1972, 1974, 1975, 1979
Jeff Gordon	4	1995, 1997, 1998, 2001

The NASCAR drivers' championship has been contested since 1949. California native Jimmie Johnson is tied at the top of the all-time wins list with seven, but his five-season streak, 2006–2010, is easily the best in the sport's history. Johnson's racing career began on 50cc motorcycles when he was just five years old. All of Johnson's NASCAR championship wins have been achieved driving Chevrolets; his current car is a Camaro ZL1. He has won eighty-three NASCAR races so far in his career but surely has more to come.

NHL team with the most Stanley Cup wins
MONTREAL
CANADIENS

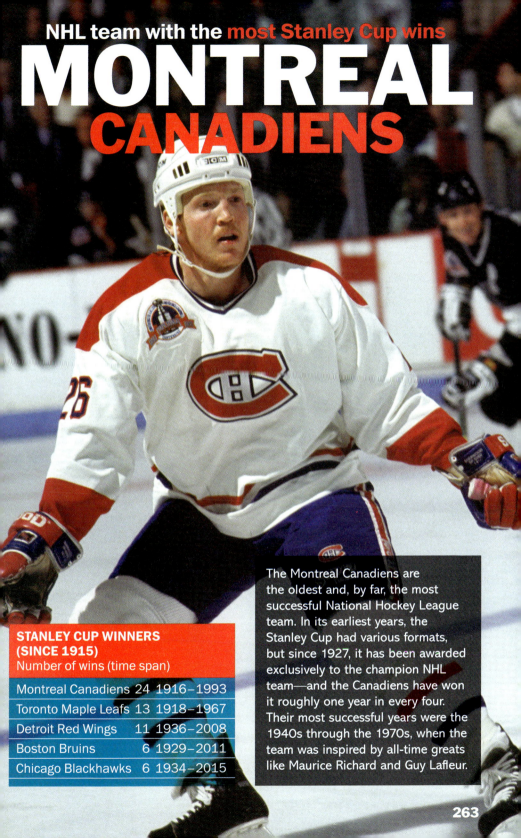

STANLEY CUP WINNERS (SINCE 1915)
Number of wins (time span)

Montreal Canadiens	24	1916–1993
Toronto Maple Leafs	13	1918–1967
Detroit Red Wings	11	1936–2008
Boston Bruins	6	1929–2011
Chicago Blackhawks	6	1934–2015

The Montreal Canadiens are the oldest and, by far, the most successful National Hockey League team. In its earliest years, the Stanley Cup had various formats, but since 1927, it has been awarded exclusively to the champion NHL team—and the Canadiens have won it roughly one year in every four. Their most successful years were the 1940s through the 1970s, when the team was inspired by all-time greats like Maurice Richard and Guy Lafleur.

Sports Stars

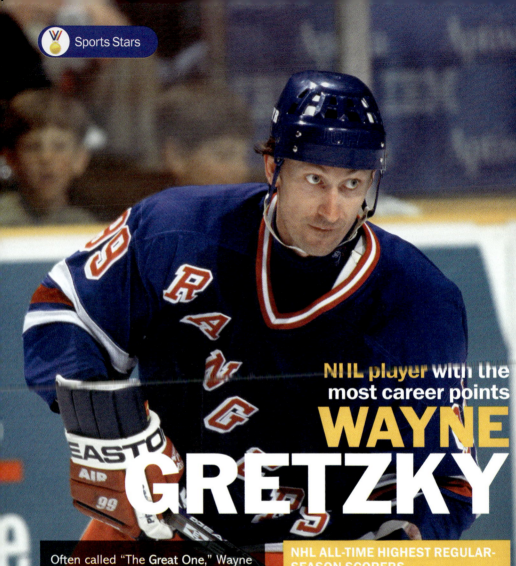

NHL player with the most career points

WAYNE GRETZKY

Often called "The Great One," Wayne Gretzky is regarded as the most successful hockey player. As well as scoring more goals and assists than any other NHL player—both in regular-season and in postseason games—Gretzky held over sixty NHL records in all by the time of his retirement in 1999. The majority of these records still stand. Although he was unusually small for an NHL player, Gretzky had great skills and an uncanny ability to be in the right place at the right time.

NHL ALL-TIME HIGHEST REGULAR-SEASON SCORERS
Number of points (goals) (career years)

Wayne Gretzky	2,857 (894)	1978–1999
Jaromír Jágr	1,921 (766)	1990–2018
Mark Messier	1,887 (694)	1979–2004
Gordie Howe	1,850 (801)	1946–1979
Ron Francis	1,798 (549)	1981–2004

first woman to play in an NHL game

MANON RHÉAUME

Manon Rhéaume had a fine career as a goaltender in women's ice hockey, earning World Championship gold medals with the Canadian National Women's Team. She is also the first—and only—woman to play for an NHL club. On September 23, 1992, she played one period for the Tampa Bay Lightning in an exhibition game against the St. Louis Blues, during which she saved seven of nine shots. She later played twenty-four games for various men's teams in the professional International Hockey League.

Sports Stars

most gold medals in world climbing competitions
JANJA GARNBRET

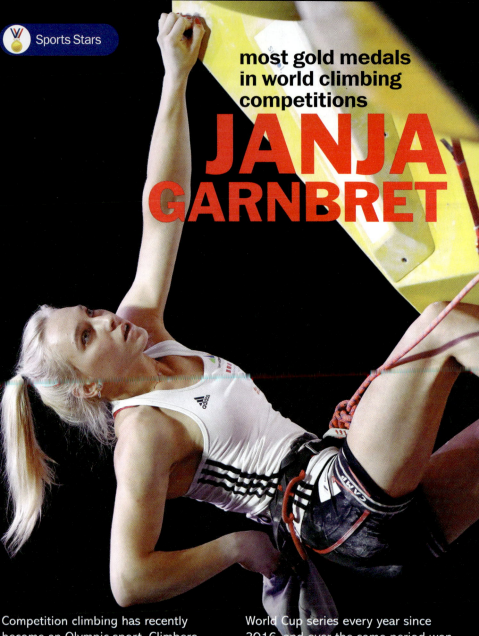

Competition climbing has recently become an Olympic sport. Climbers compete on indoor climbing walls in three disciplines—lead climbing, speed climbing, and bouldering—to arrive at a combined score for a medal. Janja Garnbret, who is from Slovenia, has won more gold medals than any other climber, male or female, in World Championships and World Cup events. She has won the combined event World Cup series every year since 2016, and over the same period won six golds at the World Championships, including all three in 2019. Jakob Schubert of Austria and Adam Ondra of the Czech Republic share the top of the men's list and are among the Olympic favorites. With the 2021 Olympics still to come at the time of writing, who will take the first-ever Olympic gold medals in this sport?

Nathan Chen made skating history at the 2018 Winter Olympics by being the first-ever skater to attempt and land six quadruple jumps during one performance. Quad jumps—in which the skater spins around four times while in the air—are among the hardest moves in skating, and grouping several of them in one program makes them more difficult still. Chen's record-breaking moves did not win a medal because he skated poorly in another part of the competition, but he won the 2018 World Championship after landing his six quads once again. He retained his title in 2019 with a world-record score and added a third world gold in 2021.

first-ever skater to land six quadruple jumps

NATHAN CHEN

Sports Stars

most Winter Olympics snowboarding gold medals
SHAUN WHITE

A professional skateboarder, successful musician, and Olympic and X Games star, Shaun White has an astonishing range of talents. He has won more X Games gold medals than anyone else, but his three Olympic golds, in the halfpipe competitions in 2006, 2010, and 2018, the most ever by a snowboarder, are perhaps his biggest achievement. The best of all was in 2018 when he landed two super-difficult back-to-back tricks in the final round to jump into first place. White's medal happened to be the USA's 100th at the Winter Olympics; that total now stands at 105, but Norway leads in that category with 132 to date.

highest pole vault
ARMAND DUPLANTIS

Born in 1999 and raised in Louisiana by an American father and Swedish mother, Armand "Mondo" Duplantis started setting pole-vault records when he was still in elementary school. After choosing to compete for his mother's homeland, he landed his first big win in adult competition in the 2018 European Championships. In 2019, he gained a silver medal in the World Championships, but in 2020 he moved ahead of the field in his event. First, he set a new world record of 6.17 meters and then improved it to 6.18 meters (20 feet 3 inches). These records were in indoor competitions, but in 2020 Duplantis also achieved the best-ever outdoor jump—6.15 meters—though this is not an official world record.

269

# Sports Stars

most medals won by an individual
MICHAEL PHELPS

Michael Phelps may be the greatest competitive swimmer ever. He did not win any medals at his first Olympics in 2000, but at each of the Summer Games from 2004 through 2016, he was the most successful individual athlete of any nation. When he announced his retirement after London 2012, he was already the most decorated Olympic athlete ever—but he didn't stay retired for long. At Rio 2016, he won five more golds and a silver, taking his medal total to twenty-eight—twenty-three of them gold.

MOST SUCCESSFUL OLYMPIANS
Number of medals won (gold)

Michael Phelps USA Swimming	2004–2016	28 (23)
Larisa Latynina USSR Gymnastics	1956–1964	18 (9)
Nikolai Andrianov USSR Gymnastics	1972–1980	15 (7)

Four athletes, Ole Einar Bjørndalen of Norway, Boris Shakhlin of the Soviet Union, Edoardo Mangiarotti of Italy, and Takashi Ono of Japan, have each won thirteen medals.

most decorated
American gymnast ever
SIMONE
BILES

Simone Biles won her first two world championship titles in 2013 at the age of sixteen and has added to her total every season since then, apart from during a career break in 2017. Biles is only four foot eight, but her tiny frame is full of power and grace, displayed most memorably in her favorite floor exercise discipline. She is so good that several special moves are named after her—and they are so difficult that she is the only competitor so far to perform these in championships. To date, she has won four Olympic and nineteen World Championship gold medals.

Sports Stars

fastest man in the world
USAIN BOLT

Jamaica's top athlete Usain Bolt is the greatest track sprinter who has ever lived. Other brilliant Olympic finalists have described how all they can do is watch as Bolt almost disappears into the distance. Usain's greatest victories have been his triple Olympic gold medals at London 2012 and Rio 2016, plus two gold medals from Beijing 2008. Usain also holds the 100-meter world record (9.58s) and the 200-meter record (19.19s), both from the 2009 World Championships.

FASTEST 100-METER SPRINTS OF ALL TIME
Time in seconds

Usain Bolt (Jamaica)	9.58 Berlin 2009
Usain Bolt (Jamaica)	9.63 London 2012
Usain Bolt (Jamaica)	9.69 Beijing 2008
Tyson Gay (USA)	9.69 Shanghai 2009
Yohan Blake (Jamaica)	9.69 Lausanne 2012

most decorated Paralympian ever
TRISCHA ZORN

Trischa Zorn is the most successful Paralympian of all time, having won an astonishing fifty-five medals, forty-one of them gold, at the Paralympic Games from 1980 to 2000. She won every Paralympic event she entered from 1980 to 1988. Zorn is blind and helps military veterans with disabilities enter the world of parasport. Zorn was inducted into the Paralympic Hall of Fame in 2012.

LEADING FEMALE PARALYMPIC MEDALISTS
Number of medals won

Trischa Zorn, USA	55
Béatrice Hess, France	25
Sarah Storey, Great Britain	25
Chantal Petitclerc, Canada	21
Mayumi Narita, Japan	20

Sports Stars

country with the most all-time Paralympic medals
USA

Although China topped the Paralympic medal table at the 2016 Summer Games in Rio (239 medals), with the United States coming in fourth (115 medals), the United States comfortably leads the all-time medal count in the Paralympic Summer Games. Norway heads the standings in the Winter Games, with the United States in second, giving the United States an overall medal total that will be unbeatable for many years to come.

COUNTRY WITH THE MOST PARALYMPIC MEDALS
Total number of medals won

United States	2,494
Germany*	1,871
Great Britain	1,824
Canada	1,220
France	1,209

* includes totals of former East and West Germany

first
Paralympic
triathlon
RIO
2016

Most people would find a 750-meter swim, followed by a 20-kilometer bike ride, then a 5-kilometer run quite challenging—but then try all that with a physical or visual impairment, too. That's how it is for paratriathletes. Sixty Paralympians qualified for the first-ever Olympic paratriathlon at Rio in 2016. Only six of the possible ten events (men and women) were contested in Rio, with the United States' two golds, one silver, and one bronze being the best national result.

Index

A

Aaron, Hank 255
Abbott Magic Company 207
Abdul-Jabbar, Kareem 246
Abu Dhabi 60
Abyssinian 152
Ace Ventura: When Nature Calls 37
Actor 27, 35, 37, 39
Actress 7, 27, 31, 34, 35, 36, 38, 45
Affleck, Ben 39
African bush elephant 116
Aircraft 56
Alabama 186
Alabama Crimson Tide 252
Alaska 187
Albertsons Stadium 197
Album, music 9, 11, 12, 14, 18, 20, 21
Aleut 187
Alligator 194
Amazon River 170
American Music Awards 21
American Shorthair 152
America's Got Talent 38
Amphitheater 190
Amusement park 208
Andes 165
Andrianov, Nikolai 270
Androgyny 6
Angel City FC 239
Angora rabbit 146
Animated movie 41, 43
Annie 34
Antarctica 139, 164
Apollo 10 spacecraft 58–59
App 90, 95, 98
Appaloosa 147
Arabian Desert 168
Arcaro, Eddie 241
Arctic 178
Arecibo Observatory 65
Argentina 157, 257
Arizona 52, 188
Arkansas 189
Arm span 118
Arowana 144
Asian elephant 116
AstroTurf 197
Austin 228
Australia 75, 109, 113, 114, 157, 167, 168, 173
Australian Open 260
Avengers: Endgame 32
Avengers: Infinity War 32

B

Baby name 87
"Baby Shark Dance" 91
Bad Boys franchise 40
Bad Bunny 20
"Bad to the Bone" school bus 50
Bald eagle 136
Ballet 209
Bar-tailed godwit 113
Barn owl 133
Barringer, Daniel Moreau 188
Barringer Crater 188
BASE jumping 233, 240
Baseball 199, 253–255
Baseball Hall of Fame 254
Basketball 239, 244–248
Bat 117, 228
Batting average 254
Battle of the Little Bighorn 226
Beagle 149
Bear 86
Beasts of the Southern Wild 34
Beatles, The 12, 14, 190
Beauty vlogger 104
Beaver Stadium 67
Bee 219
Beetle 121
Behnken, Bob 49
Bellamy, Will 185
Beluga sturgeon 169
Ben Afquack 145
"Best I Ever Had" 12
Beyoncé 19
Bicycle 49
Biden, Joe 184
Big cat 122
Big Toyz Racing 52
Bigelow, Kathryn 33
Biles, Simone 271
Billboard charts 12, 16, 20
Billboard Music Awards 13
Billy Elliot: The Musical 44
Biltmore House 218
Binz 81
Bird 113, 133–139, 145, 185
Bird, Larry 245
Bjørndalen, Ole Einar 270
Black Lives Matter 48
Black Panther 24, 32
Black Rock Desert 54
Black Widow 25
Black-footed ferret 109
Blacktip shark 129
Blake, Yohan 272
Bleymaier, Gene 197
"Blinding Lights" 8
Bloodhound 54
Blue whale 127
BMW Kenny 109
Bolivia 69
Bolt, Usain 121, 272
Bombel 147
Bonds, Barry 255
Borneo 132
Boseman, Chadwick 24
Boston Breakers 259
Boston Bruins 263
Boston Celtics 245
Boston Red Sox 253

Botswana 120
Bowser, Muriel 48
Box office 32, 40, 41, 43
Brady, Tom 250, 251
Brazil 179, 257
Brazilian wandering spider 140
Breda 75
Brees, Drew 250
Brick 64
Bridge 74, 181, 228, 233
Bristlecone pine 158
Bristol, Rhode Island 224
British Shorthair 152
Broadway shows 42–44
Brooks, Garth 14
Brown, Barnum 211
Brown, Millie Bobby 31
Bryant, Kobe 238, 246, 247
BTS 7, 13
Bugatti 51
Bull shark 129
Bulldog 149
Bullock, Sandra 36
Burj Khalifa 70–71, 240
Burundi 170

C

Cable Guy, The 37
Cactus 133
California 50, 108, 158, 159, 174–175, 177, 184, 190
California redwood 159
Call of Duty 90, 101
Call of Duty: Black Ops Cold War 99
Cambodia 144
Cambridge Medical Robotics 105
Campbell, Brad and Jen 52
Canada 64, 75, 153, 274
Candy 192
Candy Crush 90
Candy Crush Saga 90
Cape Canaveral 59
Capitol building 205
Car 51, 54
Career points 246, 248, 264
Carey, Mariah 17
Carlin Trend 213
Carolina Reaper 225
Carrey, Jim 37
Caspian Sea 169
Castle 80–81
Cat 97, 152–153
Catchings, Tamika 248
Cathedral 80
Cats 42
Cave 162–163
Caviar 169
Celebrity 88
Centodieci 51
Champ 144
Chance the Rapper 7
Change.org petition 93
Charles, James 94
Chattanooga Bakery 227

276

Chauvin, Derek 93
Cheetah 120
Chen, Nathan 267
Chernow, Ron 44
Chicago 42
Chicago Blackhawks 263
Chicago Bulls 239, 245
Chihuahua 151
Chile 73, 165
Chili pepper 225
China 55, 66, 72, 74, 78–79, 166, 170, 242, 274
Chiron Super Sport 300+ 51
Chomolungma 166
Church 80, 217, 224
Cincinnati Red Stockings 199
Cincinnati Zoo 120
Cinnamon roll 222
"Circle of Life" 43
Citi Field 108
Citystars 73
Clash of Clans 90
Climate change 167, 172, 173, 175, 176
Climbing 166, 266
Coast Douglas-fir 159
Coastal Carolina Chanticleers 197
Cobb, Ty 254
Cocoa powder 64
Coldplay 11
Colon 207
Colorado 177, 191
Colugo 115
Connecticut 192
Coral reef 157, 167
Corgi 149
Country music 17, 18
Country Music Awards 18
Country Music Hall of Fame 18
Court, Margaret 260
COVID-19 pandemic 30, 31, 40, 42, 64, 86, 87, 99, 108–109, 112, 156, 184, 193, 202, 256
Crab 193
Crater of Diamonds 189
Crawfish 203
Crayola Experience 223
Crayon 223
Crazy Horse Memorial 226
Crew Dragon 49
Cripps, Donald 233
Crocodile 132, 194
Cross Island Chapel 217
Cruise ship 82
Crystal Lagoons 73
Cunningham, Jeff 256
Currie, Smokin' Ed 225
Cutworm moth 141
Cyrus, Billy Ray 17
Czech Republic 80

D

Dachshund 149

Daddy Yankee 10
Dahl, Roald 45
Dam 221
D'Amelio, Charli 95
Dance 91, 95, 209
"Dance Monkey" 8
Dance, Thomas 205
Danyang-Kunshan Grand Bridge 74
Day, Pat 241
Dead Sea 164
Delahanty, Ed 254
Delaware 193
Demetriou, Cleo 45
Dengue fever 142
Denman Glacier 164
Desai, Binish 64
Desert 168
Desert Dome 212
"Despacito" 10, 17
Despicable Me franchise 41
Detroit Red Wings 263
Detroit Tigers 254
Devon Rex 152
Diamond 189
Diesel, Vin 39
Dill, Howard 160
DiMaggio, Joe 253
Diner 215
Dinosaur 127, 157, 211
Director, movie 24, 33
Disney+ 25
Disneyland 108
Divide 11
Divo 51
Djokovic, Novak 261
Do-dodonpa 60
Dog 96, 144, 148–149, 151
Dog Bark Park Inn 69
Dolphin 129
Donovan, Landon 256
"Don't Start Now" 8
Dr. Seuss' How the Grinch Stole Christmas 37
Draco 115
Dragon, robotic 106–107
Dragonfly 143
Dragon's Breath 225
Drake 12
"Drivers License" 7
Dubai 66, 70–71, 240
Duck 145
Dumb and Dumber 37
Dun, Joshua 15
Dungen, Thomas van den 81
Duplantis, Armand 269
DuPont, Margaret Osborne 260
Dupree, Candice 248
"Dynamite" 7

E

Eagle 136
Eagles, The 14
Ear 116
Earnhardt, Dale, Sr. 262

Earnings 11, 16, 31, 38–39, 41, 43, 95, 99
Earth Day 156
Easton 223
Eden Project 77
Egg 137, 139, 143
Egypt 73, 83
Eight Hundred, The 40
Eilish, Billie 16
El Tatio 165
El Último Tour del Mundo 20
Elephant 116
Elevator 200
Elf owl 133
Elk 191
Emerson, Roy 261
Eminem 19
Emmy Awards 27
Emperor penguin 138–139
Empire State Building 231
Encephalitis 142
Enchilada 216
Enola Holmes 31
Estrada, Roberto 216
"Euphoria" 13
Evans, Nathan 6
Everest 166
Everest, Sir George 166
Everglades National Park 194
evermore 9
Excuse Me, I Love You 16
Exotic Shorthair 152
Eyak 187

F

Face mask 64
Facebook 173
Fake news 87
The Falcon and the Winter Soldier 25
Fall, Albert 232
Fanny 106–107
Favre, Brett 250
Fearless 9
Feathers 135
Federer, Roger 261
Fenelon Place Elevator 200
Ferrari World 60
Ferret 109
FIFA Soccer 101
FIFA Women's World Cup 258
FIFA World Cup 257
"Filter" 13
Fireworks 202
Fish 128–129, 144, 169
Florida 75, 136, 151, 194
Flower 156
Floyd, George 93
Flying fish 115
Flying lemur 115
Flying lizard 115
Flying squid 115
Flying squirrel 115
folklore 9, 21
Fonsi, Luis 10, 17, 91

277

Index

Football 30, 197, 249–252
Football field 197
Forest City 199
"Formation" 19
Formula Rossa 60
Fort Wayne 199
Fossil 193, 211
Fourth of July 224
France 51, 73, 257, 261, 274
Franchesca 146
Franchise, movie 32, 36, 40–41
Franchise, videogame 101
Francis, Ron 264
Freestanding building 72
French Bulldog 149
French Open 260
Frog 131
Frozen II 41
Fruit 160
Fugen, Fred 240
Fundraiser 173

G

G-force 60
Gabeira, Maya 171
Gabriel, Peter 19
Gadot, Gal 30, 39
Galápagos penguin 139
Game Boy 100
Game show 28
Games console 86, 100
Garden, vertical 76
Garnbret, Janja 266
Gas station 232
Gastrodia agnicellus 156
Gay, Tyson 272
General Earth Minerals 189
Gentoo penguin 139
Georgia, Eurasia 162
Georgia, USA 195
German Shepherd 144, 149
German Short-haired Pointer 149
Germany 81, 257, 258, 274
Geyser 165
Giant huntsman spider 140
Giant Pumpkin European Championship 160
Giant sequoia 159
Ginsburg, Ruth Bader 185
Giraffe 113, 124–125
Giza 83
Gizmo 145
Glacier 164
Glider 115
Global warming 167, 172, 175, 176
Globe skimmer 143
Goat 108
Godwit 113

Gold 213
Golden eagle 136
Golden Globe awards 29, 34
Golden Retriever 149
Golden silk orb-weaver 140
Golden State Warriors 245
Goliath bird-eating tarantula 140
Gomez, Dalton 16
Gomez, Selena 88
Gordon, Jeff 262
Gorilla 112, 118
Grammer, Kelsey 26
Grammy Awards 21
Grand Prismatic Spring 235
Grand Slam 260–261
Grand Theft Auto 101
Grande, Ariana 16, 88
Graves, J.K. 200
Great Barrier Reef 167
Great Britain 53, 77, 108, 274
Great gray owl 133
Great Salt Lake 229
Great Sphinx 83
Great Victoria Desert 168
Great Wall of China 242
Great white shark 129
Greater Philadelphia Expo Center 102
Green city 75
Green wall 76
Greenhouse 64, 77
Greenhouse gas 172, 176
Gretzky, Wayne 264
Grimes 87
Grint, Rupert 25
Guinness World Records 49, 96, 97, 102, 103, 145, 238
Guns N' Roses 11
Gymnastics 270, 271

H

Haas, III, Eduard 192
Hailstone 180
"Hakuna Matata" 43
Hale, Sarah Josepha 206
Hamilton 44
Hamilton, Alexander 44
Hamilton Field 199
Hamm, Mia 259
Hamwi, Ernest 210
Harmony 55
Harris, Kamala 184
Harry Potter 25, 32
Hartack, Bill 241
Hashtag 92, 185
Hawaii 196
Hawking, Stephen 26
Heaven Sent Brandy 151
Hell Creek Formation 211
Henry, Justin 35
Henry Doorly Zoo 212
Hess, Béatrice 273
Hillary, Sir Edmund 166
Hillenburg, Stephen 25

Himalayas 166, 240
Hoatzin 134
Hoffman, Dustin 35
Holly, Lauren 37
Home runs 255
Honey 219
Hong Kong 66, 82
Honolulu 196
Hornsby, Rogers 254
Horse 147
Horse-racing 241
Horsefly 141
Horseshoe crab 193
Hot spring 235
Hotel 68–69
Hotel Palacio de Sal 69
"Hotline Bling" 12
How Ridiculous 244
Howe, Gordie 264
Howler monkey 123
Huddleston, John Wesley 189
Hungarian sheepdog 148
Hunger Games 36
Hunt, Richard Morris 218
Hurley, Doug 49
Hurricane 172, 173
Hurricane Arthur 172
The Hurt Locker 33
Hveravellir 165
Hyperion 159

I

"I Want to Hold Your Hand" 14
Ice hockey 263–265
Ice sculpture 173
Ice skating 267
Ice cream cone 210
Iceland 165
Idaho 69, 165, 197
If You're Reading This It's Too Late 12
Illinois 198
Illusionist 94
Imanbek 8
India 64, 67, 132, 181
Indiana 199
Indonesia 130
Ingram, Kerry 45
Insect 121, 141, 142–143
Instagram 25, 88, 92, 96–97, 145, 157
International Ballet Competition 209
International Hockey League 265
International soccer caps 259
International Space Station 49
Inuit 187
Iolani Palace 196
Iowa 200
iPhone gaming app 90
Ishaqbini Hirola Community Conservancy 113
Italo 55
Italy 55, 257

278

J

Jackson, Michael 21
Jackson, Shoeless Joe 254
Jágr, Jaromir 264
Jaguar 122
James Bond movie franchise 32
James, LeBron 246, 247
Japan 49, 55, 60, 86, 258
Jenner, Kylie 88
Jeopardy! The Greatest of All Time 28
Jiffpom 96
Jockey 241
Johnson, Dwayne (The Rock) 39, 88
Johnson, Jimmie 262
Johnson, Magic 245
Jolie, Angelina 38
Jonathan 150
Jones, Bobby 195
Joon Ho, Bong 24
Jordan, Michael 239, 246
Jordan Rift Valley 164
Juventus 88

K

K-pop 7
K2 166
Kagera River 170
Kalahari Desert 168
Kalakaua, King 196
Kamara, Kei 256
Kamchatka 165
Kanchenjunga 166
Kangaroo Island 113
Kansas 201
Kansas City Chiefs 30
Kaohsiung City 76
Kekiongas 199
Kentucky 202
Kentucky Derby 202, 241
Kenya 113
Keyhole surgery 105
Khury, Gui 238
Kiely, Sophia 45
King, Billie Jean 260
King penguin 139
King, Zach 94
Kingda Ka 60
Kitti's hog-nosed bat 117
Koala 114
Komodo dragon 130
Komondor 148
Korra 25
Kramer vs. Kramer 35

L

La Voiture Noire 51
Labrador Retriever 149
Lady Gaga 19
Lafleur, Guy 263
Lake 169, 170, 173, 221, 229
Lake Erie 173
Lake Huron 169
Lake Michigan 169

Lake Superior 169
Lake Victoria 169, 170
Landmine 144
Las Vegas 52
Last Dance, The 239
Latynina, Larisa 270
Laurence Olivier Awards 45
Lawrence, Jennifer 36
Lawrence, Martin 40
Leaf 161
Led Zeppelin 14
Legend of Korra, The 25
LEGO® 82
Lemonade 19
Lemur 115
Leopard 122
Leroux, Gaston 42
Les Misérables 42
Lesotho 244
"Level of Concern" 15
Levy, Dan 27
Levy, Eugene 27
LGBTQIA+ 25
Lhotse 166
Liar Liar 37
Lied Jungle 212
"Life Goes On" 13
Lightning 174, 179
Lil Nas X 17
Liliuokalani, Queen 196
Lilly, Kristine 259
Lincoln, Abraham 206
Lincoln Park Zoo 198
Lion 120, 122
Lion King, The 42, 43
Lipa, Dua 8
Little owl 133
Lizard 130
Llama 145
Llandudno 108
Lloyd, Carli 259
Lloyd Webber, Andrew 42
Locust 141
London 59, 108
Long-whiskered owlet 133
Lopez, Jennifer 16
Los Angeles Hollywood Bowl 190
Los Angeles Lakers 238, 245
Louisiana 203
Lover 9
Lover's Deep 69
Lufa Farms 64

M

Macaroni penguin 139
McCarthy, Melissa 38
McDormand, Frances 33
Madagascar 156
Madonna 19
Maezawa, Yusaku 89
Magawa 144
Magic 207
Maglev train 55
Maine 204

Maine Coon Cat 152
Major 144
Makalu 166
Malaria 142
Maletsunyane Falls 244
Mall of America 208
Malone, Karl 246
Mandrill 119
Mangiarotti, Edoardo 270
Manning, Peyton 250
Maple syrup 230
Maradona, Diego 88
Mardi Gras 186
Mariana Trench 164
Mario franchise 101
Mario Kart 101
Mars 48
Mars rover 48
Marvel Cinematic Universe 25, 32
Maryland 205
Maryland State House 205
Masked Singer, The 30
Massachusetts 205, 206
MASSIV 61
Matilda 45
Mawsynram 181
Mays, Willie 255
Mesoamerican Barrier Reef 167
Messi, Lionel 88
Messier, Mark 264
Meteor Crater 188
Methuselah 158
Mexican free-tailed bat 228
Mexico 128, 133, 151
Michigan 67, 207
Michigan Stadium 67
Michigan Wolverines 252
Microsoft 102
Migration 113, 128, 143
Milwaukee Bucks 246
Minecraft 102–103
Minefaire 2016 102–103
Minions 41
Minitrailer 53
Minnesota 145, 208
Miracle Milly 151
Miranda, Lin-Manuel 44
Mississippi 209
Mississippi–Missouri River 170
Missouri 147, 210, 218
Mitchell, Earl, Sr. 227
Mite 121
MLB 253–255
MLS 256
Mobility scooter 53
Modern Family 38
Moderna 109, 184
Monkey 119, 123
Mononofu 49
Monster school bus 50
Monster truck 52
Montana 211
Montana, Joe 249
Montreal Canadiens 263

279

Index

Moon 59
Moon Person trophy 19
MoonPie 227
Moreno, Jaime 256
Mosquito 142
Moss, Randy 249
Moth 141
Motorcycle 192
Mount Everest 166
Mount Rushmore 226
Mount Shasta 177
Mountain 166, 240
Mountain ash 159
Movies 24, 25, 32–41
MTV Movie Awards 36–37
MTV Video Music Awards 19
Mudbug 203
Multiple-arch dam 221
Murphy, Annie 27
Musas 104
Museum 59, 108, 195, 196, 211, 215, 232
Museum of the Rockies 211
Music video 7, 10, 15, 19
Musicals 42–45
Musk, Elon 87
My People, My Homeland 40
"My Time" 13
Myanmar 117
Myers, Mike 37

N

Nadal, Rafael 261
Nagumo, Masaaki 49
Nala Cat 97
Nansen Ski Club 214
Narendra Modi Stadium 67
Narita, Mayumi 273
Narwhal 126
NASA 48, 56, 57, 58
NASCAR 227, 262
National Geographic 157
National Historic Landmark 196
National Natural Landmark 201
National Park 165, 191, 194, 235
National Women's Soccer League 239
Native Americans 187
Navratilova, Martina 260
Nazaré 171
NBA 245–247
NCAA 248
Nebraska 212
Nepal 166
Nest 136
Netflix 29, 39, 239
Netherlands, the 65, 75, 77, 258
Nevada 52, 54, 213
New Caledonia Barrier Reef 167
New Century Global Center 72
New England Patriots 251

New Hampshire 205, 214
New Jersey 60, 205, 215
New Mexico 216
New Orleans Saints 250
New River Gorge Bridge 233
New York 66, 108, 145, 173, 217, 218, 243
New York Yankees 253
New Zealand 113, 165
NFL 249–251
NHL 263–265
Nickelodeon 25, 91
Nickelodeon Universe 208
NikkieTutorials 104
Nile River 170
Ningaloo Reef 167
Ninja Giant 157
Nintendo DS 100
Nintendo Switch 98
No. 1 album 12, 20
No. 1 single 6, 7, 12, 17
Nock, Freddy 243
Nomadland 33
North American elf owl 133
North Carolina 218
North Dakota 219
North Korea 67
Norway 75, 258, 268, 274
Norway spruce 158
Notre Dame Fighting Irish 252

O

Oakland Athletics 253
Ocasio, Benito Martinez 20
O'Doul, Lefty 254
Office building 231
O'Hara, Catherine 27
Oheka Castle 218
Ohio 60, 67, 220
Ohio Stadium 67
Oklahoma 179, 221
Old Faithful 165
"Old Town Road" 17
"Old Town Road – Remix" 17
Olivia Hope Foundation 31
Olympic Games 248, 266, 267, 268, 270–275
Ondra, Adam 266
One Direction 6
"One Sweet Day" 17
Oneida 217
Ono, Takashi 270
Orakei Korako 165
Orangutan 112
Orchid 156
Oregon 159, 222
Oscars 24, 30, 33–35
Oslo 75
Ostrich 120, 137
Otter 112
Owens, Terrell 249
Owl 133, 185

P

Pajitnov, Alexey 98

Pakistan 73
Palacio de Sal 69
Papua New Guinea 135
Paralympians 273–275
Paralympic Hall of Fame 273
Parasite 24
Paratarsotomus macropalpis 121
Paratriathlon 275
Parker Solar Probe 57
Parton, Dolly 184
Pass completions 250
Pattinson, Robert 36, 37
Pearce, Christie 259
Pelé 257
Penguin 138–139
Pennsylvania 67, 223
Pensacola Dam 221
Pensmore 218
Pentagon 72, 231
People's Dispensary for Sick Animals 144
Pepper X 225
Perseverance 48
Persian cat 152
Persson, Markus 102
Petit, Philippe 243
Petitclerc, Chantal 273
Petty, Richard 262
PEZ candy 192
Phantom of the Opera, The 42
Phelps, Michael 270
Philadelphia Zoo 198
Phoenix Mercury 248
Pilgrims 206
P!nk 16
Pittsburgh Pirates 255
Planetary rover 48
PlayStation 2 100
PlayStation 5 86
Plymouth 206
Poison dart frog 131
Pokémon 101
Pokémon GO 90
Polar bear 198
Pole vault 269
Pomeranian 96
Pondexter, Cappie 248
Pons, Lily 190
Poodle 149
Portman, Natalie 239
Possum 113
PPE 64
Prague Castle 80
Presley, Elvis 14
Primate 118
Producers, The 44
Prometheus 158
Pronghorn 120
Puerto Rico 65, 151
Pujols, Albert 255
Pumpkin 160
Pygmy possum 113
Pyongyang 67
Pyramid 83, 162

280

Q

Qin Shi Huang 78–79
QTvan 53
Quadruple jumps 267
Queen 196
Queen's Gambit, The 29

R

Ra sun god 83
Rabbit 146
Ragdoll 152
Railroad 200
Rainfall 181
Rain forest 212
Rap 7, 12, 20
Rapinoe, Megan 258
Rashford, Marcus 239
Rat 144
Red Force 60
Red Notice 39
Redwood 159
Reffet, Vince 240
Rennert Mansion 218
Reptile 132
Reputation 9
Retweet 24, 89
Reynolds, Ryan 39
Rhéaume, Manon 265
Rhode Island 224
Ribbon-tailed astrapia 135
Ricch, Roddy 8
Rice, Jerry 249
Richard, Maurice 263
River 170
Rivers, Philip 250
Robinson, Jackie 195
Roblox 90
Robot 49, 86, 105–107, 157
Rock City 201
Rock concretion 201
Rockefeller Center 185
Rocky 185
Rocky Mountain National Park
  191
Rodrigo, Olivia 7
Rodriguez, Alex 255
Roller coaster 60
Rolling Stones 11
Ronaldo, Cristiano 88
Rose Bowl 252
"Roses (Imanbek Remix)" 8
Rottweiler 149
Royal Botanical Gardens 156
Royal palace 196
Rozov, Valery 240
Rungrado 1st of May Stadium 67
Russia 165
Ruth, Babe 253, 255

S

Sagarmatha 166
Sahara desert 168
SAINt JHN 8
St. Louis Blues 265
St. Louis Cardinals 253

St. Louis World's Fair 210
St. Vitus Cathedral 80
Sakakibara Kikai 49
Salar de Uyuni 69
Salt 69
Saltwater crocodile 132
Saltwater lake 229
Sampras, Pete 261
San Alfonso del Mar 73
San Antonio Spurs 245
San Diego Chargers 250
San Francisco 49ers 30, 249
San Francisco Giants 253,
  255
San Jose Earthquakes 256
Sand Sculpture Festival 81
Sandcastle 81
Sande, Earl 241
Sandler, Adam 37
Savi's pygmy shrew 117
Scaffolding 77
Schitt's Creek 27
Schlitterbahn Galveston
  Waterpark 61
Schmidt Ocean Institute 157
School bus 50
Schubert, Jakob 266
Science Museum, London 59,
  108
Scomberomorus 56
Scottish Fold 152
Sculpture 65, 81, 83, 173, 226
Sea shanty 6
*Sgt. Pepper's Lonely Hearts
  Club Band* 14
Shakhlin, Boris 270
Shanghai Maglev 55
Shark 128–129
Sharm el-Sheikh 73
Sheeran, Ed 11, 26
Shenzhen 66
Ship 82
Shoemaker, Bill 241
Shopping mall 72, 208
Shrek franchise 41
Shrew 117
Siberia 122, 178
Silver Lake 177
Silverstone, Alicia 36
Simpsons, The 26
Sin City Hustler 52
Sinclair, Christine 259
Singapore 75
Singer, female 16
Sitka spruce 159
Skateboarding 238, 242
Skiing 214, 234
Skowhegan State Fair 204
Skyscraper 66, 70–71
Sleep 114
Smell 134
Smith, Emmitt 249
Smith, Katie 248
Smith, Maggie 25
Smith, Will 37, 40, 109

Snow leopard 122
Snowboarding 268
Snowfall 177
Snowy owl 133
Soccer 67, 88, 239, 256–259
Solar probe 57
"Soon May the Wellerman
  Come" 6
South Carolina 225
South Dakota 180, 226
Southdale Center 208
Soviet Union 98, 270
Spacecraft 48, 49, 57, 58–59
SpaceX 49, 87
Spain 55, 60
Sphynx cat 152, 153
Spider 140
SpongeBob SquarePants 25
Sports Hall of Fame 195
Spotify 7, 8, 20
Springbok 120
Sprinting 272
Squid 115
Squirrel 115
Stadium 67, 197
Stanley Cup 263
Star, Jeffree 104
Star Wars 32
State fair 204
"Stay" 13
Steel arch bridge 272
Stevens, Gary 241
Stewart, Kristen 36
Stinkbird 134
Storey, Sarah 273
Stork 136
Storm 172, 173, 174
Strait, George 18
Stranger Things 31
Streaming 7, 8
Streep, Meryl 35, 38
Sturgeon 169
Styles, Harry 6
Submarine 68
Sun 57
Super Bowl 8, 30, 249, 251
Super Bowl LIV 30
Super Mario World 101
Surfing 171
Surgical robot 105
Sweden 158
Swift, Taylor 9, 16, 21
Swimming 270
Swimming pool 73
Swiss Alps 243
Switzerland 64
Sydell Miller Mansion 218
Sydney 75
Symphony of Lights 66
Syrian Desert 168

T

Talgo 55
Taiwan 76
Tamarack 177

281

Index

Tamaulipas pygmy owl 133
Tampa 75
Tampa Bay Buccaneers 251
Tampa Bay Lightning 265
Tarantula 140
Tasmania 159
Taurasi, Diana 248
Taylor-Joy, Anya 29
Teapot Dome Service Station 232
Telescope 65
Temperature extremes 172, 178
Tennessee 18, 184, 227
Tennis 260–261
Tenzing Norgay 166
Terra-cotta warriors 78–79
Tetris 98
Tevis, Walter 29
Texas 61, 185, 228
Thailand 73, 117
Thanksgiving celebration 206
The Weeknd 7, 8
Theme park 60
Thompson, Tina 248
Thrust SSC 54
Thumbelina 147
Thunder Over Louisville 202
Tidel 166
Tiger 122
Tiger beetle 121
Tiger shark 129
Tightrope walk 243
TikTok 6, 8, 17, 94–95, 109
Titanosaur 127, 157
Toltec civilization 151
Tomb 78–79
Tomlin, Chris 190
Tomlinson, LaDainian 249
Tones and I 8
Tongue 125
Tony Awards 44, 45
Top Thrill Dragster 60
Tornado 173
Toronto Maple Leafs 263
Tortoise 150
Touchdowns 249
Tour, music 11, 16
Train 55, 65
Trebek, Alex 28
Tree 158–159
Treepedia 75
Triathlon 275
Trinidad Moruga Scorpion 225
Triple Crown 241
Turkey 146
Turtle 185
Tusk 126
TV show 25–30

Twenty One Pilots 15
Twilight franchise 36
Twitter 7, 24, 87, 89, 144
Tyrannosaurus rex 211
Tyus, Wyomia 195

U

U2 11
Uganda 112
Umbrella 181
UNICEF 31
Universal Studios 41
University of Connecticut Huskies 248
University of Southern California 252
Unpiloted plane 56
Uruguay 257
US Open 260
USA 14, 144, 149, 173, 175, 258, 259, 268, 274, 275
  see also individual states
USC Trojans 252
Utah 229

V

Vaccination center 108
Vaccine 108, 109
Valley of Geysers 165
Vancouver 75
Vanderbilt, George 218
Velaro 55
Vergara, Sofía 38
Verkhoyansk 178
Vermont 230
Versius 105
Veryovkina Cave 162–163
Viaduct 74
Vice president 184
Video game 98–103
Video Music Awards 19
Videoconference 87
Ville Saint-Laurent 64
Virginia 205, 231
Vivian 180
Vlogger 104
Vonn, Lindsey 239

W

Wade, Lestat 102
Wahlberg, Mark 39
Wales 108
Wallis, Quvenzhané 34
WandaVision 25
Warwick, Dionne 7
Washington 48, 232
Washington, George 205
Washington Olympics 199
Water coaster 61
Water lily 161
Wave 171
Way, Danny 242

West Nile virus 142
West Virginia 233
Whale 65, 127, 129
Whale shark 128
Wheelie 49
White, Shaun 268
White House 144
White stork 136
Whole Enchilada Fiesta 216
Wight, Rev. Henry 224
Wildfire 113, 173, 174–175, 178
Willemijns, Mathias 160
Williams, Serena 239, 260
Wimbledon 260
Wingspan 117, 136
Winter Olympics 267, 268
Winter X Games 242
"Wipe It Down" 109
Wisconsin 234
WNBA 248
Wolf, robotic 86
Wolferman's Bakery 222
Women's rights 220
Wondolowski, Chris 256
Woodley, Shailene 36
Working day 220
World Dream 82
World Series 253
World Trade Center 243
Worldloppet 234
Worthington-Cox, Eleanor 45
Wyoming 165, 235

X Æ A-12 87
X Games 238, 242, 268
X-43A plane 56
X-Men: Apocalypse 36

Y

Yangtze River 170
Yellow fever 142
Yellow River 170
Yellowstone National Park 165, 235
Yes Man 37
YHLQMDLG 20
YouTube 7, 10, 91, 104, 157
Yup'ik 187
Yuya (Mariand Castrejón Castañeda) 104

Z

Zambelli Fireworks 202
Zhao, Chloé 33
Ziolkowski, Korczak 226
Zoella 104
Zonda HP Barchetta 51
Zoo 109, 112, 120, 198, 212
Zoom 87
Zorn, Trischa 273

282

Photo Credits

Photos ©: cover top left: Album/Alamy Stock Photo; cover top right: JMEnternational for BRIT Awards/Getty Images; cover center: Emilee Chinn/Getty Images; cover background: Vertigo3d/Getty Images; back cover top left: Sipa USA/Alamy Live News; back cover bottom left: Sipa USA/Alamy Live News; back cover bottom right: Ringo Chiu/ZUMA Wire/Alamy Live News; 4–5, 13: ABC/Shutterstock; 5 top right and throughout: calvindexter/DigitalVision Vectors/Getty Images; 6 top: Matt Winkelmeyer/MG19/Getty Images for The Met Museum/Vogue; 6 center: Historia/Shutterstock; 6 bottom: OfficialCharts.com/Shutterstock; 7 top: Getty Images for Children's Diabetes Foundation; 7 center: Avalon/Newscom; 7 bottom: Theo Wargo/Getty Images for The Recording Academy; 8: Kevin Mazur/Getty Images for TW; 9: Jay L Clendenin/Los Angeles Times/Shutterstock; 10 background: Petra Urbath/EyeEm/Getty Images; 10 center: GDA via AP Images; 11: RMV/Shutterstock; 12: Jonathan Short/Invision/AP Images; 14 background: Blue67/Dreamstime; 14 center: AP Images; 15: MARKA/Alamy Stock Photo; 16: Jordan Strauss/Invision/AP Images; 17: John Shearer/Getty Images for The Recording Academy; 18: Rick Diamond/WireImage/Getty Images; 19: Kevin Mazur/WireImage/Getty Images; 20: Victor Chavez/Getty Images for Spotify; 21: Kevin Mazur/AMA2019/Getty Images; 22–23, 27: PictureLux/The Hollywood Archive/Alamy Stock Photo; 23 top right and throughout: Aratehortua/iStock/Getty Images; 24 center: Richard Shotwell/Invision/AP Images; 25 top: Photo 12/Alamy Stock Photo; 25 center: Thibaud MORITZ/Abaca Press/Sipa USA via AP Images; 25 bottom: Album/Alamy Stock Photo; 26: PictureLux/The Hollywood Archive/Alamy Stock Photo; 26 background: zaricm/Getty Images; 28: Eric McCandless via Getty Images; 29: Album/Alamy Stock Photo; 30: JOHN ANGELILLO/UPI/Shutterstock; 32 background: Gaudilab/Dreamstime; 32 top: BFA/Alamy Stock Photo; 33: Chris Pizzello/Pool/Shutterstock; 34: Jim Smeal/BEI/Shutterstock; 35: AF archive/Alamy Stock Photo; 36 top: Featureflash/Dreamstime; 37: Matt Sayles/AP Images; 38: Xavier Collin/Image Press Agency/Sipa USA via AP Images; 39: Frank Masi/Warner Bros/Kobal/Shutterstock; 40: TCD/Prod.DB/Alamy Stock Photo; 41: Photo 12/Alamy Stock Photo; 42 top: Jimmyi23/Dreamstime; 42 bottom: Simon Fergusson/Getty Images; 43: ROSLAN RAHMAN/AFP via Getty Images; 44: Bruce Glikas/FilmMagic/Getty Images; 45: Nick Harvey/WireImage/Getty Images; 46–47: NASA's Goddard Space Flight Center; 47 top right and throughout: Turqay Melikli/iStock/Getty Images; 48 top: NASA/JPL-Caltech; 48 center: CARLOS VILAS DELGADO/EPA-EFE/Shutterstock; 49 top: Aflo Co. Ltd./Alamy Stock Photo; 49 center: Bruno Wittwer/www.wheels4nepal.ch; 49 bottom: NASA/SpaceX; 50: Jeffrey Greenberg/UIG via Getty Images; 51 wheel: Jonathan Woodcock/DigitalVision Vectors/Getty Images; 52: Brad and Jen Campbell/Barcroft/Barcroft Media via Getty Images; 53: Jonathan Hordle/REX/Shutterstock; 54: David Taylor/Allsport/Getty Images; 56: NASA; 57: NASA/Johns Hopkins APL; 58–59: NASA; 60: Iain Masterton/age fotostock; 61: Schlitterbahn Waterparks and Resorts; 62–63, 68: Oliver's Travels; 63 top right and throughout: photosynthesis/iStock/Getty Images; 64–65: Niels Wenstedt/BSR Agency/Getty Images; 64 top: SEBASTIEN ST-JEAN/AFP via Getty Images; 64 center: Roman Sandoz/Moment/Getty Images; 64 bottom: Courtesy of Dr. Binish Desai; 65 top: RICARDO ARDUENGO/AFP via Getty Images; 66: Yinwei Liu/Moment/Getty Images; 67: Eric Lafforgue/Art In All Of Us/Corbis via Getty Images; 69: Palacio de Sal; 70–71: WIN-Initiative/Stockbyte Unreleased/Getty Images; 72: Beercates/Dreamstime; 73: Crystal Lagoons/REX/Shutterstock; 74: Imaginechina Limited/Alamy Stock Photo; 75 main: ZUMA Press Inc/Alamy Stock Photo; 75 circle: bubaone/Getty Images; 77: Jon Spaull/age fotostock; 78–79: Chederros/age fotostock; 80: Kajanek/Dreamstime; 81: Jens B'ttner/picture-alliance/dpa/AP Images; 82: Edward Wong/South China Morning Post via Getty Images; 83: domin_domin/E+/Getty Images; 84–85, 109 top: LESZEK SZYMANSKI/EPA-EFE/Shutterstock; 86 center: Aflo/Shutterstock; 87 center: ANGELA WEISS/AFP via Getty Images; 88: Pedro Fiúza/NurPhoto via AP Images; 89: Aflo/Shutterstock; 91: Leon Neal/Getty Images; 93: Erik McGregor/LightRocket via Getty Images; 94: gotpap/Bauer-Griffin/GC Images/Getty Images; 95: Jay L Clendenin/Los Angeles Times/Shutterstock; 96: The Photo Access/Alamy Stock Photo; 97: Amanda Edwards/WireImage/Getty Images; 98: Normadesmond/Dreamstime; 100: Asiaselects/Alamy Stock Photo; 101: Stephen Lam/Getty Images; 102–103: theodore liasi/Alamy Stock Photo; 104: Edgar Negrete/Clasos/LatinContent/Getty Images; 105: CMR Surgical; 106–107: Andreas Muehlbauer, Furth im Wald; 108–109: Peter Byrne/PA Wire via AP Images; 108 top: Jeff Gritchen/MediaNews Group/Orange County Register via Getty Images; 109 center: USFWS Mountain Prairie; 109 bottom: Pablo Cuadra/WireImage/Getty Images; 110–111, 140: Piotr Naskrecki/Minden Pictures; 111 top right and throughout: photosynthesis/iStock/Getty Images; 112–113: Ben Curtis/AP Images; 112 center: Pairi Daiza Zoo/Cover Images via AP Images; 113 top: manwithacamera.com.au/Alamy Stock Photo; 113 center: WILDLIFE GmbH/Alamy Stock Photo; 113 bottom: Ondrejprosicky/Dreamstime; 114: Marius Sipa/Dreamstime; 115: Nicholas Bergkessel, Jr./Science Source; 116: Steve Bloom Images/Superstock, Inc.; 117: Steve Downeranth/Pantheon/Superstock, Inc.; 118: NHPA/Superstock, Inc.; 120 main: Gallo Images/The Image Bank/Getty Images; 120 icons: Krustovin/Dreamstime, Alenaopt2013/Dreamstime, filo/DigitalVision Vectors/Getty Images, Wectors/Dreamstime, D_A_S_H_U/iStock/Getty Images; 121: Dr. Samuel J.S. Rubin (W.M. Keck Science Center, Pitzer College) and Dr. Jonathan C. Wright (Department of Biology, Pomona College), The

283

Photo Credits

Claremont University Consortium, Claremont, CA, USA; 122: Tom Brakefield/DigitalVision/Getty Images; 123: Jesse Kraft/Dreamstime; 124–125: WLDavies/Getty Images; 126: Bryan & Cherry Alexander/Science Source; 127: Franco Banfi/WaterFrame/age fotostock; 128: Joanne Weston/Dreamstime; 129: Tobias Friedrich/WaterFrame/age fotostock; 130: Ksumano/Dreamstime; 132: William D. Bachman/Science Source; 133: Jim Zipp/ardea.com/age fotostock; 134: nikpal/Getty Images; 135: Tim Laman/Minden Pictures; 136: Chris Knightstan/Pantheon/Superstock, Inc.; 137: Fabian Von Poser/imageBROKER/Shutterstock; 138–139: Bernard Breton/Dreamstime; 141: Stephen Dalton/Minden Pictures/Superstock, Inc.; 142: Roger Eritja/age fotostock; 143: Saurav Karki/iStock/Getty Images; 144–145: Official White House Photo by Adam Schultz; 144 top: Genlady/Dreamstime; 144 center: PDSA/Cover Images via AP Images; 145 top right background: RapidEye/E+/Getty Images; 145 duck: Catchyimages/Dreamstime; 145 bottom right: Chrisbrignell/Dreamstime; 146: Dr. Betty Chu; 147: Grzegorz Michalowski/EPA-EFE/Shutterstock; 148: Mary Altaffer/AP Images; 149: Isselee/Dreamstime; 150: mark phillips/Alamy Stock Photo; 151 background: Hsc/Dreamstime; 152: Isselee/Dreamstime; 154–155, 174–175: Carlos Avila Gonzalez/The San Francisco Chronicle via Getty Images; 156–157: Matt Rourke/AP Images; 155 top right and throughout: Cajoer/Dreamstime; 156 bottom: Johan Hermans; 157 center: Photo courtesy of Schmidt Ocean Institute; 157 bottom: Pablo Gallina; 158: p-orbital/Getty Images; 159: Andrei Gabriel Stanescu/Dreamstime; 160: THOMAS KIENZLE/AFP via Getty Images; 161: SuperStock/age fotostock; 162–163: Robbie Shone; 164: Operation IceBridge/NASA; 165: Idamini/Alamy Stock Photo; 167: Auscape/Universal Images Group via Getty Images; 168: Valentin Armianu/Dreamstime; 169: NASA image by Jeff Schmaltz, MODIS Rapid Response Team; 170: Image Source/Getty Images; 171: Armando Franca/AP Images; 172–173: LUKAS COCH/EPA-EFE/Shutterstock; 172 top: Maynor Valenzuela/Getty Images; 173 top: Lisa Maree Williams/Getty Images; 173 center: Jeffrey T. Barnes/AP Images; 173 bottom: David J. Phillip/AP Images; 176: Imaginechina/Newscom; 177: CampPhoto/Getty Images; 178: LYagovy/iStock/Getty Images; 179: VectorPocket/iStock/Getty Images; 180: Nadine Spires/Dreamstime; 181: Amos Chapple/Shutterstock; 182–183, 187: Joe Raedle/Getty Images; 183 top right and throughout: Djahan/iStock/Getty Images; 184–185: Official White House Photo by Chuck Kennedy; 184 bottom: PictureLux/The Hollywood Archive/Alamy Stock Photo; 185 top: Erik Pendzich/Shutterstock; 185 center: U.S. Navy; 185 bottom: Ravensbeard; 186: Dan Anderson via ZUMA Wire/Newscom; 188: Russ Kinne/age fotostock; 190: EuroStyle Graphics/Alamy Stock Photo; 191: aznature/Getty Images; 192: Randy Duchaine/Alamy Stock Photo; 193: Newman Mark/age fotostock; 194: Michael S. Nolan/Alamy Stock

Photo; 196: Lucy Pemoni/AP Images; 197: Steve Conner/Icon SMI/Corbis via Getty Images; 199: Buyenlarge/Getty Images; 200: Don Smetzer/Alamy Stock Photo; 201: Keith Kapple/Superstock, Inc.; 202: Stephen J. Cohen/Getty Images; 203: John Cancalosi/Pantheon/Superstock, Inc.; 204: Diane Labombarbe/DigitalVision Vectors/Getty Images; 205 banners: RUSSELLTATEdotCOM/DigitalVision Vectors/Getty Images; 209: Richard Finkelstein for the USA IBC; 210: Historic Collection/Alamy Stock Photo; 211: Edgloris E. Marys/age fotostock; 212: Robert_Ford/Getty Images; 213: REUTERS/Alamy Stock Photo; 214: Nansen Ski Club; 215: Loop Images/UIG via Getty Images; 216: Visit Las Cruces; 217: Tina Pomposelli; 218: Alan Marler/AP Images; 218 icons: siraanamwong/iStock/Getty Images; 220: Library of Congress; 221: John Elk III/Lonely Planet Images/Getty Images; 222: Courtesy of Wolferman's Bakery™; 223: Matt Rourke/AP Images; 224: Jerry Coli/Dreamstime; 225: Ed Currie/PuckerButt Pepper Company; 226: Sergio Pitamitz/age fotostock; 228: Fritz Poelking/age fotostock; 229: Christian Heeb/age fotostock; 230: Tara Golden/Dreamstime; 232: Kevin Schafer/Photolibrary/Getty Images; 234: PAUL M. WALSH/AP Images; 235: Richard Maschmeyer/age fotostock; 236–237, 269: Oleksii/MODJ/PressFocus/Shutterstock; 237 top right and throughout: Dmstudio/Dreamstime; 238–239: Jae C. Hong/AP Images; 238 bottom: REUTERS/Alamy Stock Photo; 239 top: ALESSANDRO DI MARCO/EPA-EFE/Shutterstock; 239 center: Chuck Berman/Chicago Tribune/Tribune News Service via Getty Images; 239 bottom: Courtesy of Angel City FC; 240: ZJAN/Supplied by WENN.com/Newscom; 241: AP Images; 242: Streeter Lecka/Getty Images; 243: Gian Ehrenzeller/EPA/Shutterstock; 244: How Ridiculous; 245: Ronald Martinez/Getty Images; 246: Focus on Sport/Getty Images; 247: Tribune Content Agency LLC/Alamy Stock Photo; 248: Elaine Thompson/AP Images; 249: Greg Trott/AP Images; 250: Dave Shopland/BPI/Shutterstock; 251: ERIK S LESSER/EPA-EFE/Shutterstock; 252: Kevork Djansezian/Getty Images; 253: Jed Jacobsohn/Getty Images; 254: Mark Rucker/Transcendental Graphics/Getty Images; 255: Denis Poroy/AP Images; 256: Scott Winters/Icon Sportswire via AP Images; 257: AP Images; 258: David Vincent/AP Images; 259: Guang Niu/Getty Images; 260: Daily Express/Hulton Archive/Getty Images; 261: Julian Finney/Getty Images; 262: Jared C. Tilton/Getty Images; 263: Bruce Bennett Studios/Getty Images; 264: Rocky Widner/Getty Images; 265: Bruce Bennett Studios/Getty Images; 266: Aflo Co. Ltd./Alamy Stock Photo; 267: MARCO BERTORELLO/AFP/Getty Images; 268: The Yomiuri Shimbun via AP Images; 270: Mitchell Gunn/Dreamstime; 271: Zhukovsky/Dreamstime; 272: Stuart Robinson/Express Newspapers via AP Images; 273: ARIS MESSINIS/AFP/Getty Images; 274: Raphael Dias/Getty Images; 275: Buda Mendes/Getty Images. All other photos © Shutterstock.com.

284

SCHOLASTIC SUMMER READING

The free Scholastic Summer Reading program motivates kids to read all summer long while helping to increase book ownership for kids with limited or no access to reading materials.

Through the fun and digitally safe program, kids are invited to visit the Scholastic Home Base Summer Zone! In the zone, they can read free e-books and enjoy author read-aloud videos, attend author events, make new friends, earn digital reading milestones and rewards, and keep Reading Streaks™ to help unlock a donation of 100,000 books from Scholastic, distributed to kids across rural America by Save the Children.

READING AMBASSADORS

Bestselling and award-winning authors including summer reading ambassadors Sayantani DasGupta (Kiranmala and the Kingdom Beyond series), Varian Johnson (*Twins, The Great Greene Heist*), Ann M. Martin (The Baby-Sitters Club series), and Kelly Yang (*Front Desk*) hosted virtual events all summer long.

SCHOLASTIC SUMMER READING

BY THE NUMBERS

18 THE NUMBER OF WEEKS KIDS PARTICIPATED IN THE SCHOLASTIC SUMMER READING PROGRAM

21 THE NUMBER OF AUTHORS WHO PARTICIPATED IN SUMMER READING EVENTS

100,000 THE NUMBER OF BOOKS DONATED TO KIDS WITH LIMITED OR NO ACCESS TO READING MATERIALS

THE THREE MOST READ BOOKS THIS SUMMER

SCHOLASTIC SUMMER READING

BY THE NUMBERS

18 THE NUMBER OF WEEKS KIDS PARTICIPATED IN THE SCHOLASTIC SUMMER READING PROGRAM

21 THE NUMBER OF AUTHORS WHO PARTICIPATED IN SUMMER READING EVENTS

100,000 THE NUMBER OF BOOKS DONATED TO KIDS WITH LIMITED OR NO ACCESS TO READING MATERIALS

THE THREE MOST READ BOOKS THIS SUMMER

SCHOLASTIC SUMMER READING

The free Scholastic Summer Reading program motivates kids to read all summer long while helping to increase book ownership for kids with limited or no access to reading materials.

Through the fun and digitally safe program, kids are invited to visit the Scholastic Home Base Summer Zone! In the zone, they can read free e-books and enjoy author read-aloud videos, attend author events, make new friends, earn digital reading milestones and rewards, and keep Reading Streaks™ to help unlock a donation of 100,000 books from Scholastic, distributed to kids across rural America by Save the Children.

READING AMBASSADORS

Bestselling and award-winning authors including summer reading ambassadors Sayantani DasGupta (*Kiranmala and the Kingdom Beyond* series), Varian Johnson (*Twins, The Great Greene Heist*), Ann M. Martin (*The Baby-Sitters Club* series), and Kelly Yang (*Front Desk*) hosted virtual events all summer long.

SCHOLASTIC SUMMER READING

Congratulations to all our summer readers! By starting and keeping Reading Streaks™, kids helped to unlock a donation of 100,000 new print books from Scholastic, distributed by Save the Children to kids with limited or no access to reading materials across rural America. Children in Cocke County, Tennessee, shown on these pages, were some of the young readers to receive free books as part of the Scholastic Summer Reading Program.

SCHOLASTIC SUMMER READING

To learn more about Scholastic Home Base and join the year-round fun, visit:
scholastic.com/homebase

SCHOLASTIC